(continued)

Reading the Visual

An Introduction to Teaching Multimodal Literacy

Frank Serafini

Foreword by James Paul Gee

TEACHERS COLLEGE PRESS

TEACHERS COLLEGE | COLUMBIA UNIVERSITY

NEW YORK AND LONDON

Published by Teachers College Press, 1234 Amsterdam Avenue, New York, NY 10027

Library of Congress Cataloging-in-Publication Data

Serafini, Frank.
Reading the visual : an introduction to teaching multimodal literacy / Frank Serafini ; foreword by Gunther Kress.
pages cm
Includes bibliographical references and index.
ISBN 978-0-8077-5471-9 (pbk. : alk. paper) — ISBN 978-0-8077-5472-6 (hardcover : alk. paper)
1. Visual literacy. 2. Visual learning. 3. Literacy—Philosophy. 4. Critical pedagogy. I. Title.
LB1068.S468   2013
370.11'5—dc23   2013025440

ISBN 978-0-8077-5471-9 (paper)
ISBN 978-0-8077-5472-6 (hardcover)
eISBN 978-0-8077-7243-0 (ebook)

Printed on acid-free paper
Manufactured in the United States of America

21   20   19   18   17   16   8   7   6   5   4   3   2

My good friend Dr. Lawrence (Larry) Sipe taught me more about picturebooks than anyone else in the world, opening my eyes to the wonders of this visual art form. His gentle way of teaching and being in the world will always remind me of what it truly means to be a scholar and friend.

Contents

PART II: CURRICULAR FRAMEWORKS AND
PEDAGOGICAL APPROACHES

Foreword

School has long been about print, words on a page and lectures that sound like print. We give students texts and when they do not understand them we give them more texts. If they do not understand a word we give them more words, such things as definitions, explications, and lectures.

The world outside school today is replete with words married to images, sounds, the body, and experiences. When we play a video game we integrate words, maps, images, actions, goals, choices, and experiences. We manipulate a surrogate body, our avatar in the game. Science books and articles today are replete with graphs, images, and diagrams. As we move to digital books, books will become media full of images, videos, simulations, games, and representations readers will be able to handle and manipulate and even build.

This new world is a multimodal world. Language is one mode; images, actions, sounds, and physical manipulation are other modes. Today, students need to know how to make and get meaning from all these modes alone and integrated together. In the 21st century anyone who cannot handle multimodality is illiterate. They must be able to handle it critically, since without critical and analytic skills a multimodal world of games, ads, news, and other media is a world where it is easier than ever to lie, scam, dupe, and manipulate people.

Multimodality is the rage today and the "new new thing." But, it seems new only because we linguists have done such a poor job analyzing language. We treat language as words and grammar. But language has never been unimodal. Language-in-use is a performance. We string words together with tone, pitch, and stress of the voice, with gestures and actions, and embodied interactions with others. We use language in contexts full of props that support meaning just as the stage and its props do in theater.

Furthermore, words do not primarily get meaning from other words. The meaning of a word is not its definition. A definition only sets a rough range of the possibilities for a meaning a word has. In actual use, words are related to images, actions, and experiences that give them meaning. So, notice if I say, "The coffee spilled, go get a mop," "The coffee spilled, go get a broom," or "The coffee spilled, go stack it again." In each case you associate an image with the word "coffee," not a definition or another string of words. This is the norm for language. We need to also remember that in school meanings need to be concrete and operational before, after lots of practice in multiple contexts, meaning becomes more abstract.

Language has always and ever been a multimodal performance. Furthermore, when we speak, write, listen, or read we can and should do so proactively. We can, when we need to, carefully design what and how we want to mean. We can read and listen critically by rewriting and repeating in our heads what we have read or heard, reflecting on it, and asking how else—maybe better—it could have been written or said.

We need these same proactive skills when we deal with media like video games. As we play we want to think about how the game is designed, how we can shape our play to take advantage of that design, and how we might have been able to modify or improve that design. More and more this sort of proactive meaning maker/giver is what schools will have to produce in our highly complex and high risk global world. Schools too often make students passive consumers of meaning, when it is their birth right to be active producers of meaning.

Frank Serafini gets it. He knows that language and literacy were our original multimodal forms. He knows that today they are as crucial as they have ever been, but that they comport with a great many new relatives that are daily widening and transforming what we mean and how we mean it.

—James Paul Gee,
Mary Lou Fulton Presidential Professor of Literacy Studies,
Arizona State University

Acknowledgments

I would like to acknowledge the following people for their friendship and support throughout the development of this project. Although this is certainly my personal labor of love, it would not have been possible without their encouragement and scholarly insights.

Gunther Kress—for the few short days you spent talking with us at University of Nevada, Las Vegas. Your ideas resonate through this text. I will always remember your description of Las Vegas as "semiotic heaven."

Mari Koerner—my dean at Arizona State University. I appreciate your willingness to allow me time away from my duties to pursue professional and personal goals.

John Nittolo, Kathyrn D'Angelo, and all the other wonderful educators I have had the pleasure to work with over the years. Your dedication to your students is unparalleled.

Carrie Matheson, Mike Oliver, and the faculty at Zaharis Elementary—the research I was able to do at your school confirmed for me the importance of these ideas for children.

My graduate students—thanks for sitting patiently in my class as I worked through these ideas. I hope I didn't ramble on too much.

Anthony Browne—thank you so much for the use of your wonderful illustrations throughout the book. Your work inspires me and has forced me to reconsider the role of visual images in picturebooks forever.

My sister Suzette—thank you for allowing me to bounce ideas off you whenever possible. You always keep me grounded in the lives and needs of students, and for this I am most humbled.

For my partner and fellow educator, Lindsey Moses—thanks for allowing semiotics into our dinner conversations. Who knew such loveliness and intelligence could be wrapped into one person? You are the most caring person I have ever met. Thanks for letting me into your life.

Reading the Visual

An Introduction to Teaching Multimodal Literacy

Introduction

Let us teach design, and let us get it out of the museums, let us get it off the pages and drawing boards, and let us put it to work.

—Robert McCloskey (1958)

From the time humans first painted images on the cave walls in Lascaux, France to the present day, when images stream across our computer screens, we have used visual images to help understand ourselves and make sense of the world around us. The creation of visual images allows us to communicate our feelings and ideas across time and space, develop relationships with one another, and document our everyday experiences. We are confronted by visual images in every aspect of our daily lives. Magazines, picturebooks, music videos, text messages, websites, billboard advertisements, textbooks, documentary films, graphic novels, and comic books are just a few of the places we encounter images in today's society.

Making sense of the world is a basic human process. As humans, we perceive the world around us through our senses, particularly our sense of sight, and use this information to understand what we are experiencing. The visual images we encounter each and every day play an important role in how we make sense of the world and how we see ourselves. We rely on visual data to decide what to buy, how to get where we are going, how we dress, who we are, and who we want to become. In today's world, visual images play a role in most everything we do.

As we go about our daily lives, we have grown so accustomed to seeing a vast array of visual material that we have to tune out much of it or we would quickly become overwhelmed. Because of this overload of visual data, we often take for granted the ways in which visual images play a role in our daily decisions and experiences. We have become desensitized to how visual images affect our thinking and how we view ourselves. In other words, visual images play an important, and often unseen role, in our developing identities.

The opening epigraph, from a speech given by the Caldecott Award-winning author-illustrator Robert McCloskey, suggests that the teaching of visual images and design has been excluded from the classroom and kept secret in the museums and art classes offered only to a select few. As far back as 1958, McCloskey called for the integration of art and visual images in the classroom and the study of the elements of design to support students' interpretive processes. As the texts students encounter in today's world grow more complex, we as educators should take McCloskey's advice to heart and put these ideas to work in our classrooms.

A MULTIMODAL WORLD

Rarely, if ever, do we encounter visual images all by themselves. The visual images we encounter are most often experienced as *multimodal ensembles,* a type of text that combines written language, design elements, and visual images. Museum displays, picturebooks, magazines, cookbooks, advertisements, and newspapers all combine visual images with written language and design elements into multimodal ensembles.

Multimodal ensembles utilize various *semiotic resources* to represent and communicate meaning potentials. The term *semiotic resource* is used here as an umbrella term to refer to the cultural tools created by people for representing and communicating meanings. Sculpture, painting, music, photography, color, and typography are all semiotic resources used in our society to convey and represent meanings in particular ways. A more detailed explanation of concepts like multimodality and semiotic resources will be provided in Chapter 4. In addition, a glossary of terms is included to provide quick access to the essential terms used throughout this book. For now, it is important to understand that visual images, written language, and design elements work individually and in concert with one another to represent meanings and convey information.

What constitutes a text, whether in print or digital format, has changed drastically since humans first pressed ink to paper. In the past few decades, the personal computer has amplified these changes and made resources available to the layperson that were once the province of commercial printing companies. Texts, once dominated by written language, are now experienced as multimodal ensembles that utilize visual images, design elements, and typographical features to communicate and represent ideas. As the formats used in the creation of multimodal ensembles evolve from print-based to digital environments, the semiotic resources available to authors, illustrators, and designers expand exponentially. Sounds effects, hyperlinks, video clips, fonts, and many other digitally based semiotic resources are readily available to communicate intentions and offer meaning potentials. As Kress (2010) has suggested, the "world told" has become the "world shown."

The premise of this book is fundamentally simple. Students encounter visual images accompanied by written language and design elements throughout their daily lives. To be successful, they need to expand their repertoire of strategies for making sense of these complex, multimodal ensembles. In order to more effectively develop students' strategies and approaches, teachers need theoretical, curricular, and pedagogical frameworks from which to draw upon. The purpose of this book is to address these challenges by providing theoretical, curricular, and pedagogical frameworks for teachers to use to help their students make sense of the visual images and multimodal ensembles they encounter in and out of school settings.

WHY TEACHERS AND LITERACY EDUCATORS SHOULD READ THIS BOOK

Before children learn how to walk and talk, they are inundated with visual images presented in picturebooks, on television, and throughout their home environments. As children grow to school age, the amount of visual images they encounter each day increases exponentially. Even before children head off to school, they require help in understanding the role of images in our society and how visual images affect the decisions they make, their emerging identities, the things they buy, and their day-to-day experiences. Before we as educators allow students to be affected by the powerful influences of today's mass media, we need to help them understand how visual images and multimodal ensembles work and the resources and techniques designers utilize to capture our attention and influence our decisions (Hobbs, 2011).

Freire (1970) suggested that people are required to read the world as well as read the word if they are to be successful citizens. I would extend his pronouncement by proposing that the world contains visual images and design elements as well as written language, and all of these communicative forms play a role in influencing our developing identities. In other words, students need to learn how to read between the borders of visual images as much as how to read between the lines of written text.

Comprehension strategies for helping students make sense of written text, for instance predicting, summarizing, inferring, and asking questions, have become an integral part of the instructional approaches in today's elementary and middle school classrooms. In fact, these cognitively based strategies have essentially dominated commercial materials and instructional approaches during the past few decades (Harvey & Goudvis, 2000; Miller, 2002). However, these cognitively based reading strategies alone will not be enough to support students as they attempt to make sense of the visual images and design elements they encounter in multimodal ensembles.

Students read different texts, in different ways, in different settings, for a number of different reasons. Reading email, text messages, museum brochures, or websites is very different from reading a classic novel. Each of these different texts requires students to utilize a variety of strategies to make sense of what they are reading. Unfortunately, the strategies necessary for making sense of visual images and multimodal ensembles have not been as prominent a feature in the language arts curriculum as they are in the lives of the students for whom the curriculum was intended (Anstey & Bull, 2006).

In too many classrooms, students are not provided with the strategies necessary to make sense of the vast array of visual images and multimodal ensembles they encounter. Most literacy programs and instructional frameworks concentrate on reading and writing language, and traditionally this may have been appropriate. The ability to work with written language is still privileged in our society and in our schools. However, the literacy instructional programs being incorporated into today's classrooms often fail to focus on the strategies necessary for comprehending visual images and multimodal ensembles. As the texts students encounter rely more and more on visual images and design features to communicate ideas and make sense of our world, our instructional approaches should focus more and more on the strategies used to make sense of visual images and the multimodal ensembles in which they are encountered.

Various researchers and educators have called for the expansion of literacy instructional frameworks to include media and visual literacy skills (Messaris, 1997; Richardson, 2009). These calls for expanding the literacy curriculum to include strategies for comprehending visual images and multimodal ensembles need to be supported by ongoing professional development to help teachers develop the skills and strategies necessary for ensuring that students are able to navigate, analyze, and interpret complex multimodal ensembles. The skills required by our students to decode print-based texts and write traditional five-paragraph essays will not be enough for the literate demands of our students' future.

WHAT INFLUENCED ME TO WRITE THIS BOOK

At numerous literacy conferences and professional development workshops, I have asked teachers to share a reading comprehension strategy that they would use to help students make sense of written text. The air is immediately filled with the hands of participants eager to share their thoughts about predicting, summarizing, or inferring. However, when I ask teachers to share a comprehension strategy for making sense of a visual image or multimodal ensemble, I am usually met with that "deer-in-the-headlights" look we try to avoid during classroom instruction or professional development workshops. Sometimes a participant will suggest, "Well, you just look at it!" Although simply looking at an image may be a good place to start, our students will need more support in learning how to interpret visual images than just being told to stare at them.

Gombrich (1961) asserted that the world we live in is becoming more visual than verbal. Fortunately, educators have begun in earnest to acknowledge the need for students to develop strategies for understanding the visual images and multimodal ensembles they encounter (Albers, 2008; Arizpe & Styles, 2003). As the new millennium unfolds, it is time for educators to focus on the visual images and multimodal aspects of the texts our students encounter, and develop the theoretical, curricular, and pedagogical structures to support our students' interpretations and analyses of these texts.

The information presented throughout *Reading the Visual* comes from a variety of fields of study, including art history, semiotics, media and cultural studies, communication studies, graphic design, typography, photography, and advertising. Unfortunately, teachers are rarely, if ever, exposed to these fields of study in their certification coursework, graduate degree programs, or professional development workshops. In order to teach students to navigate, comprehend, analyze, and critique the visual images and multimodal ensembles they encounter, we as educators need to go beyond the traditional boundaries of literacy pedagogy to investigate the strategies and knowledge developed in other fields and disciplines (Serafini, 2012).

Art history, semiotics, cultural and visual studies, and visual anthropology all have theoretical frameworks and analytical procedures for interpreting visual images. It would not be practical to expect classroom teachers to master such a vast array of information. However, I have spent the past 10 years researching visual literacies across a wide range of perspectives, incorporating ideas from outside traditional educational disciplines to help me rethink the foundation of my theoretical, curricular, and pedagogical frameworks. I will discuss aspects of these other fields and disciplines when they are useful in expanding our understandings of visual images and multimodal ensembles.

Drawing on my extensive experience as a classroom teacher, teacher educator, and literacy researcher, and my continued involvement in the professional development of teachers throughout North America and beyond, I can suggest an array of perspectives and instructional practices that have proven to be successful in my own classroom and with classroom teachers with whom I am currently working. When appropriate, I will share additional resources for exploring other theoretical, curricular, and pedagogical perspectives in greater detail.

In previous publications, I have written extensively about the Reading Workshop and the assessments, interactive discussion strategies, and lessons in comprehension that support readers' comprehension of written and multimodal texts (Serafini, 2001, 2004, 2009, 2010a, 2010b). In *Reading the Visual*, I will draw upon my experiences to help teachers expand their instructional practices to address visual images and multimodal ensembles, in both print-based texts and digital environments. My goal is to provide teachers with a framework that incorporates visual images and multimodal ensembles in a way that does not pose an additional burden to teachers dealing with an already burgeoning curriculum.

One of the most universally read multimodal ensembles in elementary classrooms is the picturebook. Because of its acceptance and students' familiarity with these books, they can be used as a way to introduce many of the concepts offered throughout this book. Picturebooks tell stories in a visual language that is rich and multileveled. These art forms are sophisticated despite their often deceptively simple appearance. Understanding the visual images and design elements, codes, and literary and artistic devices that have influenced the production and interpretation of picturebooks, enhances students' ability to appreciate and comprehend the subtleties of these multimodal ensembles. The more students experience these multimodal ensembles, the more they learn to appreciate the systems of meanings used in their creation.

With all the changes in the texts students encounter, how will teachers support their students' educational experiences in these rapidly changing times? What resources are readily available for helping teachers expand their knowledge base when their professional lives are extremely busy? How do teachers incorporate strategies for making sense of visual images and multimodal ensembles without dismissing their traditional literacy curriculum requirements? What pedagogical approaches are most efficient and effective for helping students make sense of the complex texts they encounter? *Reading the Visual* is designed to address these challenges in a way that makes sense to literacy educators and classroom teachers.

HOW THIS BOOK IS ORGANIZED

Part I of *Reading the Visual* lays out the foundational and theoretical concepts teachers will draw upon to understand how visual images and multimodal ensembles work. It is my assertion that quality instructional approaches are based on a solid foundation of theoretical understandings. Therefore, we need to consider not only what we do as literacy educators, but also the theoretical frameworks upon which we base our instructional decisions. In Part I, I present my tripartite analytical framework for thinking conceptually about how we can approach and interpret multimodal ensembles. This framework serves as a heuristic device for organizing the curricular and pedagogical approaches outlined in the following sections.

Part II focuses on the important role picturebooks can play in literacy education and makes a case for the inclusion of these multimodal ensembles across grade levels. Part II also presents a curricular framework for working with multimodal ensembles in educational settings. The curricular framework is comprised of three phases: (1) exposing students to multimodal ensembles, (2) exploring the features and structures of multimodal ensembles, and (3) engaging with these ensembles as producers and consumers. To demonstrate how the units of study are organized in Part III, Part II also includes a pedagogical template that will be used to develop the units of study offered in Part III.

The units of study presented in Part III will focus on ten different types of multimodal ensembles. Postmodern, wordless, historical fiction and informational picturebooks comprise the first four units of study. Other units of study focus on graphic novels, comics, cartoons, and illustrated novels. In addition, units of study focusing on news reports, advertisements, film, and digital media are included. Each unit of study contains suggestions for selecting cornerstone texts and visual images, launching the unit, lesson plans and learning experiences, text sets, analysis guides, and further resources. These units are simply examples of the types of learning experiences I have used with my students over the years and can be readily adapted to fit the needs of students in a variety of settings and grade levels. Consider these units of study as flexible outlines and recommendations for developing units of one's own.

Reading the Visual is intended as a practical resource that provides an optimal blend of instructional approaches and conceptual understandings for literacy educators to draw upon as they begin to address visual images and multimodal ensembles in their classrooms. If the world told has become the world shown, our students will need a new set of strategies for comprehending what they are being shown.

The theories and learning experiences suggested in this text provide an array of strategies for considering the various images and multimodal ensembles we encounter in our everyday lives. I believe it is time to provide literacy educators and their students with the competencies necessary for successfully engaging with a world dominated by visual images and multimodal ensembles. I hope you find this book as rewarding to read as it has been to write.

Part I

THEORETICAL AND INSTRUCTIONAL FOUNDATIONS

1

Multimodal Ensembles

There are no exclusively visual sites. All cultural sites that involve imagery include various ratios of other communicative modes and many employ more than vision.

—Paul Duncum (2004)

Whether we have called them *multimodal ensembles* or not, humans have created and shared texts that include visual images, graphic designs, and written language for hundreds of years. Egyptians used visual images and hieroglyphs to adorn their temples and burial sites. Artists from around the world have included titles and written descriptions with their visual artworks. Monks created *illuminated texts* by adding colorful designs and *historiated initials,* oversized letters at the beginnings of paragraphs, to medieval codices using gold, silver, and other precious materials. Renaissance scholars, in particular Leonardo da Vinci, used drawings to enhance their written observations and scientific notebooks.

In the early days of the printing press, texts were dominated by written language because the inclusion of black and white images in printed texts was very expensive and time-consuming. In order to print black and white visual images in these texts, artists carved images onto plates to which ink could be applied. Mass produced texts that included color images were only possible during Gutenberg's time if someone painstakingly colored in individual pages by hand. The process required special skills on the part of the artist and print maker to include visual images in commercial and religious texts.

No one could have imagined back then how easy it would become to reproduce paintings, photographs, and other visual images and incorporate them into books, magazines, and picture books, let alone foresee the advent of digital publishing. Nowadays we simply drag and drop an image into a digital text, and then add music or sound effects to it. In digital environments, visual images, sound effects, video clips, and written text are all rendered through the same basic code (digital bytes), making it relatively simple to join them together in a variety of multimodal configurations. What was once a process intended for specially trained designers and print makers has become available to the layperson through the advent of the personal computer. With a computer, some relatively inexpensive software, an Internet connection, and a printer, the average person can produce an extensive array of multimodal ensembles, including newsletters, calendars, weblogs, podcasts, and photo albums in the comfort of their own home, and make them available to millions of people through the World Wide Web.

Due to advances in technology, the creation and dissemination of texts with visual images and sophisticated design features has become commonplace. However, it is not just the incorporation of visual images into written texts that is the focus of much of today's research into visual literacies. What is of growing interest is how visual images work alongside written language and design elements, and how readers make sense across the various components and features of these ensembles. Design elements, visual images, and written language work in different ways to convey meaning and communicate information. We interpret visual images and design elements differently than we interpret written language; a picture may be worth a thousand words, but a thousand words are not the same as a picture.

We continue to draw upon visual images with increased frequency to make sense of our world, often overshadowing the once dominant role of written language. Kress (2003) asserts that we can no longer treat language as the sole or major means of representing communication and language alone cannot provide access to a meaning potential that equals that of the multimodally constructed text. This has important implications for literacy education. We need to understand what a multimodal ensemble is, how it is constituted, and how meaning is articulated and interpreted within and across various modes and multimodal elements.

SO WHAT EXACTLY IS A MULTIMODAL ENSEMBLE?

A *mode* is a system of visual and verbal entities created within or across various cultures to represent and express meanings. Photography, sculpture, painting, mathematics, music, and written language are examples of different *modes*. Every mode has a different potential for expressing and communicating meaning, and was created to serve a particular purpose within a culture. Therefore, a *multimodal ensemble* is a text composed of more than one *mode*. Artists, writers, and graphic designers utilize a variety of modes to tell stories, share information, and communicate with readers.

The term *multimodal* is often used as an adjective to describe a particular type of text. In these instances, the term refers to texts that utilize a variety of modes to communicate or represent concepts and information. A multimodal *ensemble* is simply another term for multimodal text. I prefer the term *ensemble* because the term *text* often connotes a predominantly print-based artifact. The term *ensemble* refers to entities composed of disparate elements or features rendered as a composite or cohesive whole. Therefore, a *multimodal ensemble* is a complex, multimodal entity that occurs in both print and digital environments, utilizing a variety of cultural and semiotic resources to articulate, render, represent, and communicate an array of concepts and information.

The concept of multimodality has come into vogue in the past several decades to address the increasing complexity of textual ensembles in print-based and digital formats. However, it should be noted that scholars have focused on multimodality for a few hundred years. One of the first reported studies of multimodality was an essay entitled "Laocoon: An Essay on the Limits of Painting and Poetry" (Lessing, 1766/1990) comparing the sculpture of the Trojan priest Laocoon to a passage in the *Aneid* by Virgil about the priest's warning not to let a giant horse designed by the Greek hero Odysseus into the city of Troy. Lessing (1766/1990) points out that both the sculpture and the passage describe the same event utilizing different modalities for different purposes; whereas sculptures can depict a particular moment of a complex story, the poem can portray the events unfolding through time. Sculpture is bound by aspects of its spatiality, while poetry (and in essence all written language) is bound by its temporal or sequential nature. From this early reported study to present-day research on multimodality, educators and researchers have attempted to understand how modes work, both individually and in multimodal ensembles.

TEXT, IMAGE, AND DESIGN

In general, the modes used in print-based multimodal ensembles fall into three categories: (1) textual elements, which include all written language; (2) visual images like photography, painting, drawings, graphs, and charts; and (3) design elements like borders, typography, and other graphic elements. These represent the basic elements used in print-based, multimodal ensembles. As the texts we encounter shift from print-based to digital or screen-based, the range of modes used in these texts expands to include sound effects, moving images, and other digitally rendered elements. It is easy to see how the complexity of multimodal ensembles expands exponentially in a digital environment.

Throughout the book, I will distinguish between *text* and *written text*. When I use the term *text*, I am referring to a cohesive entity that can be disseminated in a number of ways, for example a picturebook, a magazine article, a photographic essay, or a website. When I use the term *written text* or *written language*, I am referring to the written language aspects of a multimodal ensemble. Written text has material form, is rendered through a particular font or typography, serves particular purposes, and is grounded in sociocultural, political, and historical contexts. In addition, the term *genre* will be used to distinguish among the distinct varieties of texts, for example a lecture, an interview, a historical fiction novel, a wordless picturebook, or an advertisement.

I use the term *visual images* throughout this book to refer to the nontextual elements featured in multimodal ensembles, for example photographs, drawings, graphs, and diagrams. For the purpose of distinguishing among visual images, written text, and design features, I will restrict my use of the term *visual images* to refer to the photographs, paintings, and other images included in multimodal ensembles.

I will use the term *design elements* to refer to borders, white space, and other graphic elements beyond the written text and visual images. The boundaries among the various elements of a multimodal ensemble remain blurry because the features of written discourse have a visual element and visual images and design features play a role in written discourse (Serafini & Clausen, 2012; van Leeuwen, 2006). However, for the sake of clarity, I will maintain the distinction among visual images, design elements, and written text throughout this book.

HOW MODES WORK

Different modes express different meanings in different ways. Some modes are essentially two-dimensional, like photography and painting, and are used in the creation of print-based ensembles, like picturebooks, magazines, and brochures. Other modes are three-dimensional, like sculpture and architecture, and would not fit between the covers of any book unless they were photographed first. Painting, photography, music, sculpture, and mathematics are all modes that express or represent meanings, and each mode can realize meanings in ways that other modes cannot. A sculpture of a dog, a story about a dog, a diagram of a dog, and a photograph of a dog all depict different aspects of *dog* in different ways. If I draw a dog running, it takes different skills and materials than if I videotape a dog running. If I try to explain the workings of a dog's digestive system, it is probably better to use a diagram than a video camera. Each mode serves different purposes and works in different ways.

All modes have material, physiological, technological, and sociocultural aspects. Spoken language has physiological dimensions, including volume, intonation, and dialect, and technological dimensions, for example how language is written down or recorded for archiving. Spoken language also has a social dimension, for instance whether language is used in an informal conversation, a university-based lecture, a family dinner conversation, or a job interview. Sculpture's physical dimensions may involve the use of clay or marble, and photography once used film and light sensitive papers to represent objects, ideas, and meanings. Photography, like other modalities, has a social dimension, for example photos can be used as evidence in a court of law or in a family photo album to remind us of the events in our lives.

One of the primary reasons that multiple modes are utilized in various ensembles is that no single mode can completely express any particular concept or meaning (Kress, 2010). Each mode has affordances and limitations and is in itself partial. Each mode does different semiotic work and communicates or represents meanings in different ways. Visual images, design graphics, written language, and photography all use different material and semiotic resources to represent meanings. The limitations and affordances of various modes will be discussed further in Chapter 4.

MULTIMODAL OR MULTIMEDIA

A distinction needs to be made between *mode* and *media*. Media (singularly medium) are the technologies used for the rendering and dissemination of texts, in particular multimodal ensembles. Television, radio, the Internet, electronic books, and DVDs are all media used in the production and dissemination of multimodal ensembles. Modes draw on semiotic resources for the articulation, representation, and interpretation of texts, whereas media draw on semiotic resources for the dissemination of texts.

To blur the distinction a bit, modes and media cut across sensory channels; its path of perception does not characterize the nature of a particular mode. For example, language can be heard, spoken, perceived visually, and touched via braille texts. It can also be disseminated through CDs, radio, television, and the Internet. As the range of available modes for articulating, representing, and interpreting texts grows, and the variety of media for disseminating texts expands, we as educators need to consider the challenges these changes represent for literacy education.

THE DISCOVERY OF THE OBVIOUS

The current research and focus on multimodal ensembles has been referred to as the "discovery of the obvious" (Stockl, 2007) because these texts have been commonplace for an extended period of time. However, what is not as obvious are the various ways researchers and theorists have worked to understand how modes work together, and how various modes interact and often contradict one another in an effort to communicate information and render narratives. There has not been a recent shift from research focusing exclusively on multimodal ensembles; rather researchers have ultimately recognized the thoroughly multimodal nature of all texts and discourses. In other words, the focus on multimodal ensembles is simply a reflection of a changing communicative landscape.

Stockl (2007) suggests that multimodality is as old as representation. Fortunately, it is gaining ground as a focus in contemporary research and literacy education because multimodal texts and visual images will continue to dominate our literate landscapes far into the future. Because of changes in technology, our society will most likely not go back to a time when written texts are distributed without accompanying visual images. For example, although it may change in form, structure, style, presentational format, and the avenues of its dissemination, the novel remains an important literary genre across generations.

As stated in the opening epigraph, visual theorists, particularly Stockl (2007), Mitchell (2005), and Duncum (2004), would assert there are no purely visual artifacts or monomodal texts. In other words, the boundary among and across modes may be blurry at times, but purely monomodal texts or discourses do not exist in reality. All texts, whether written, oral, or hyper-textual, blend more than one mode in their creation. Discussing modes as individual and separate entities may be helpful in delineating their attributes, affordances, and limitations in academic essays, but these modes do not exist as separate entities in social practices.

Another way to consider the range of written text and visual image components of multimodal ensembles would be to envision a continuum representing a range of the multimodality of texts from textually dominant texts to visually dominant texts (see Figure 1.1).

This continuum asserts that, although there are no purely monomodal texts, there are differences among the composition of multimodal ensembles and the array of modes they draw upon. Some multimodal ensembles draw more on written language and some draw more on visual images. Written language, visual images, and design elements should not be conceptualized as mutually exclusive. Rather, what is worthy of our attention is how these modes work within and across ensembles to construct meaning potentials.

WHY SHOULD EDUCATORS CARE ABOUT MULTIMODAL TEXTS?

As the medium of the page turns to the medium of the screen, the texts that children encounter will only grow more complex (Kress, 2010). In order to create an informed and literate citizenry, readers must be able to navigate, interpret, design, and interrogate the written, visual, and design elements of multimodal ensembles. Drawing upon theories and research outside the traditional discipline of reading or literacy education will help teachers expand the strategies and skills students need in order to successfully read the textual, visual, and design elements of the multimodal texts they encounter.

Readers are confronted with multimodal ensembles that include visual images and a variety of graphic design elements in their everyday lives with greater frequency than texts that focus on written language (Fleckenstein et al., 2002). Paul Duncum (2004) states, ". . . there is no avoiding the multimodal nature of dominant and emerging cultural sites" (p. 259). Images and texts are being combined in unique ways, and students in today's world need new skills and strategies for constructing meaning in transaction with these multimodal ensembles as they are encountered during the sociocultural practices of interpretation and

Figure 1.1. Multimodal Continuum

Textually Dominant	Blended Structures	Visually Dominant
Traditional Novels	Picturebooks	Photography
Essays	Magazines	Painting
Lectures	Webpages	Sculpture
Legal Documents	Graphic Novels	Architecture
Speeches	Newspapers	Wordless Picturebooks

representation (Serafini, 2009). In order to support students' development of the skills necessary for success in modern times, teachers need to develop units of study that focus attention on these ensembles and create lessons that help students make sense of these complex texts.

Unfortunately, as many students progress through school they are expected to read more print-dense texts. Most young children's first experiences as readers are with multimodal ensembles, often picturebooks, which are dominated by visual images. When children reach school age, they are invited to read and interpret multimodal ensembles that draw upon visual images as much as written text. However, as children work their way through the grades, they are expected to focus more on written language because the texts they are required to read rely less on visual images. By the time readers reach high school and college, the print-based novel and scholarly essay dominates their reading lives.

Educational contexts have been dominated by the mode of written language and the medium of the printed text. Students that are successful at manipulating printed text, meaning they are proficient readers and writers of traditional texts, tend to be successful in today's schools. Unfortunately, one's ability to sculpt, do photography, or design comic books does not generally translate into success in public schools. A focus on written language to the exclusion of visual images may be problematic given the multimodal nature of modern communication.

Hull and Nelson (2005) assert, "multimodality can afford, not just a new way to make meaning but a different kind of meaning" (p. 225). If children are to understand how images represent and construct meaning, they need knowledge of the visual meaning-making systems used in their production. Bearne (2003) states, "children deserve to be given the key to translating their inner text making into coherent communications by explicit discussion of variations in the structures, purposes, and effects of multimodal as well as written texts" (p. 99).

Without a theoretical and pedagogical framework and associated *metalanguage* or vocabulary for comprehending and analyzing multimodal ensembles, educators will struggle to prepare students to design and interpret these complex texts. A *metalanguage* refers to a set of terms for describing and analyzing a particular mode or system of meaning (for example photography, written language, film, or painting) contained in multimodal ensembles. Before teachers can help support students as creators and interpreters of multimodal ensembles, they first have to become more familiar with these terms and concepts themselves and develop a more extensive knowledge base from which to expand their literacy curriculum.

CONCLUDING REMARKS

As multimodal texts become the norm rather than the exception in today's schools, educators need to expand their own knowledge to support students' ability to design, interpret, and utilize multimodal texts in a variety of settings. We need to accept the evolution of the texts our students encounter, and can no longer hide our heads in the sand and focus our literacy instructional practices exclusively on decoding written language. A focus on print-based texts, to the exclusion of multimodal ones in educational contexts, privileges certain forms of meaning and knowledge (Anstey & Bull, 2006). We should embrace the multimodal ensembles and pop cultural artifacts our students' experience and expand our own knowledge base concerning literacy and multimodality if we expect to expand the literate lives of our students.

2

Visual Literacy, Media Literacy, and Multiliteracies

A reason for choosing [the term] visual literacy is that it is convenient in the absence of anything better.

—John Elkins (2008)

As the opening epigraph suggests, definitions of visual literacy are anything but simple and universally accepted. Various disciplines, such as art history, semiotics, anthropology, photography, literacy education, and cultural studies all shade their definitions of visual literacy in different ways. The differences across various definitions have emerged because of changes in beliefs and theories, the different perspectives behind diverging definitions, and challenges to earlier theories and epistemologies.

Before attempting to define the term *visual literacy*, it might serve to have a working definition of *literacy* itself. The term has been defined in many different ways and has a long history in educational contexts. Although literacy per se is not the primary focus of this book, I offer a brief overview of this term to help us move forward in understanding the concepts of visual literacy, media literacy, and multiliteracies.

DEFINING LITERACY

Traditionally, the word *literacy* has referred to a set of cognitive skills that individuals acquire to function in society, primarily the ability to read and write to a specified degree of proficiency. However, more recent definitions of literacy suggest it is as much a social practice as it is an individual cognitive skill. This change in how literacy is defined suggests that literacy is something individuals *do* in particular social contexts, rather than simply something that individuals *acquire* (Gee, 1996; Street, 1995).

Au (1993) asserted that literacy is the ability and willingness to use reading and writing to construct meaning from the printed text in ways that meet the requirements of a particular social context. This definition suggests that people may be considered literate in one setting, say in a high school English class, and not in another setting, say the computer lab. It also suggests that there are different types of literacy and each one is associated with particular settings, actions, identities, and social practices.

Lemke (1998) asserted that literacy cannot be defined more precisely than "a set of cultural **competencies** for making socially recognizable meanings by the use of particular material technologies" (p. 283). In moving toward a more socioculturally oriented definition of literacy, Gee (1996) argued that literacy is concerned with situated actions and perspective taking, not simply one's ability to read and write to a certain degree of proficiency. Barton, Hamilton, and Ivanic (1999) offered a summary of sociocultural perspectives on literacy, asserting that literacy is best understood as a set of social practices patterned by social institutions and power relationships, embedded in broader social goals and cultural practices, and historically situated to accommodate new processes of sense making. In summary, being literate requires one to be able to use the various modes of representation to make sense of the world and convey meanings in particular social contexts for particular social purposes.

What was once conceptualized as an individual's acquisition of a set of cognitive skills is now viewed as a contextually grounded array of social practices enacted in particular settings for particular social purposes. In much the same way that the concept of literacy has evolved from a cognitive perspective to a socioculturally oriented one, so have the theories of visual and media literacies to which we now turn.

VISUAL LITERACY

Because the centuries-old domination of written language texts is being challenged by the rise in importance of the visual image, a focus on visual literacy has come to the fore in literacy research and instruction. Mitchell (1994) has described a *pictorial turn*, a complex transformation occurring across fields of inquiry, asserting that visual images are not fully explicable based on linguistic models of written language. A focus on multimodality needs to move beyond linguistic models to incorporate frameworks based on visual grammar and composition. His pictorial turn established the fields of visual culture and visual studies as legitimate academic disciplines concerned with multimodality and other hybrid forms of communication.

Avgerinou (2009) labels the pervasiveness of visual images in the mass media as the *Bain d'Images Era*, or era of the *image bath*, referring to the inundation of visual images in contemporary environments. She warns, however, that constantly being confronted by visual images does not necessarily lead to a "conscious recognition of this phenomenon" (Avgerinou, 2009, p. 28). The proliferation of visual images does not guarantee that students are paying any more attention to their visual environments, nor does it suggest that their ability to navigate, interpret, or analyze images is expanding to meet the demands of contemporary society.

As an additional caveat, Avgerinou (2009) warns against "living by the erroneous assumption that what has long been known as 'print culture' still rules the domains of human thought, attitude, and emotion, and still dictates the form of their expression" (p. 28). Continuing to view the world through linguistic and print-based sensibilities limits one's experiences and narrows the forms of expression and interpretation available in today's expanding visual culture. Visual literacy is complex, and multidimensional, and defined across a range of cognitive and aesthetic dimensions.

Although theorists and educators working in the field of visual studies have found it difficult to reach a consensus in defining visual literacy, it is important to understand the history of the term *visual literacy* in order to elucidate the tensions in this ongoing endeavor. John Debes, who worked for Eastman Kodak and published a newsletter entitled *Visuals Are a Language*, coined the term *visual literacy* to refer to the strategies and skills one needs to make sense of visual images (Debes, 1968). Fransecky and Debes (1972), in their initial attempts to define visual literacy, stated visual literacy is "the group of vision competencies a human being can develop by seeing and at the same time having and integrating other sensory experiences. The development of these competencies is fundamental to normal human learning" (p. 7). They saw *vision competencies* as individually developed cognitive abilities that were used for understanding visual images regardless of the contexts of their production, reception, and dissemination. These early definitions of visual literacy focused on the ability to decode, interpret, create, question, challenge, and evaluate texts that communicate with visual images as well as words, and the ability to use images in a creative and appropriate form to express particular meanings.

Theorists working to expand the definition of visual literacy combined psychological theories of perception with the sociocultural aspects of visual design and social semiotics (Chauvin, 2003). More contemporary definitions have suggested that visual literacy should be reconceptualized as a set of acquired competencies for producing, designing, and interpreting visual images and messages addressing the various contexts in which images are viewed and the production and distribution of images. Selected definitions of visual literacy from recent decades are presented in Figure 2.1.

Avgerinou and Pettersson (2011), through a review of relevant research and theorizing toward a consensus definition of visual literacy, suggested a composite theory of visual literacy needs to be comprised of the following five conceptual components:

1. visual perception,
2. visual language,
3. visual learning,
4. visual thinking, and
5. visual communication.

Figure 2.1. Definitions of Visual Literacy

- Visual literacy includes a group of skills enabling an individual to understand and use visual images for intentionally communicating with others (Ausburn & Ausburn, 1978).
- Visual literacy is the gaining of knowledge and experience about the workings of the visual media coupled with a heightened conscious awareness of those workings (Messaris, 1994).
- Visual literacy refers to a group of largely acquired abilities, that is, the abilities to understand (read), and to use (write) images, as well as to think and learn in terms of images. (Avgerinou, 2009)
- Visual literacy involves developing the set of skills needed to be able to interpret the content of visual images, examine social impact of those images and to discuss purpose, audience, and ownership. It includes the ability to visualize internally, communicate visually, and read and interpret visual images. Visual literacy also involves making judgments of the accuracy, validity and worth of images. A visually literate person is able to discriminate and make sense of visual objects and images, create visuals, comprehend and appreciate the visuals created by others, and visualize objects in their mind's eye. To be an effective communicator in today's world, a person needs to be able to interpret, create, and select images to convey a range of meanings (Bamford, 2003).

In addition, Avgerinou (2009) identified *points of convergence* among theorists attempting to define visual literacy (p. 29). An abbreviated version of these characteristics is presented in Figure 2.2.

Although early definitions of visual literacy often focus on individual cognitive abilities, visual literacy is being reconceptualized as a social practice as much as an individual, cognitively based ability or set of competencies. Sturken and Cartwright (2001) assert "meanings are produced not in the heads of the viewers so much as through a process of negotiation among individuals within a particular culture, and between individuals and the artifacts, images, and texts created by themselves and others" (p. 4). Definitions of visual literacy, therefore, should focus not only on an individual's perceptual and cognitive abilities, they should include how visual images function in broader sociocultural contexts, and how *practices of looking* inform our lives and identities (Sturken & Cartwright, 2001).

In a further attempt to expand the definition of visual literacy, Rose (2001) proposed a critical visual methodology, informed by critical theories and cultural studies, that is founded on "an approach that thinks about the visual in terms of the cultural significance, social practices and power relations in which it is embedded; and that means thinking about the power relations that produce, are articulated through, and can be challenged by, ways of seeing and imaging" (p. 3). In moving toward a critical visual methodology, Rose (2001) suggests that teachers

Figure 2.2. Defining Visual Literacy—Points of Convergence

- Visual literacy is a cognitive ability, but also draws on the affective domain.
- Visual literacy is described as an ability, skill, and competency.
- Visual literacy includes the ability to write (encode) and read (decode) visual communication.
- Visual literacy skills are learnable and teachable.
- Visual literacy skills are not isolated from other sensory skills.
- Visual literacy incorporates theories from a variety of fields of inquiry.

and students take images seriously, think about the social conditions and effects of visual objects, and consider our own way of looking at images.

Visual discourse analysis, proposed by Albers (2007), combines aspects of discourse analysis (Fairclough, 1995), social semiotics (Hodge & Kress, 1988), and the grammar of visual design (Kress & van Leeuwen, 1996) to analyze the structures and conventions within visual texts and how social identities get played out in their production. This approach conceptualizes the visual text as a communicative event that acts as a force on viewers to encourage particular actions or beliefs (Albers, 2007).

As we begin to incorporate written language, design features, and visual images into multimodal ensembles, our working definition of visual literacy needs to expand to accommodate social as well as cognitive practices for making sense of these ensembles. In attempting to bridge this theoretical terrain, my working definition of visual literacy is as follows:

Visual literacy is the process of generating meanings in transaction with multimodal ensembles, including written text, visual images, and design elements, from a variety of perspectives to meet the requirements of particular social contexts.

I know that is quite a bit to consider. However, a couple of terms and concepts require further explanation before proceeding. First, being visually literate is a social *and* cognitive process, not simply a discrete set of skills that are accumulated by individuals to apply as needed. The ability to act in a visually literate manner changes over time and context, and requires people to be able to flexibly enact a set of social practices to make sense of the images and multimodal ensembles they encounter. Second, visual literacy is about the *process* of generating interpretations from the meaning potentials available when transacting with visual images and multimodal ensembles. It is an ongoing process, not a static set of discrete skills. Third, being visually literate requires the ability to work across a *variety of modes*, including photography, painting, sculpture, diagrams, and film, not just written language. In addition, my definition suggests readers need to consider multimodal ensembles and visual images from a variety of theoretical perspectives, for example feminist, critical, sociocultural, political, historical, and aesthetic perspectives. Finally, it assumes that the immediate sociocultural contexts in which images are produced and disseminated play a central role in the meanings constructed and shared. In other words, being visually literate is about being able to make sense of the images and multimodal ensembles encountered in various settings using a variety of lenses to interpret and analyze their meaning potentials.

In later chapters, I will bring together these various theoretical perspectives when presenting an analytical framework that blends cognitive perspectives with structural, social, and ideological dimensions for interpreting visual images and multimodal ensembles (Serafini, 2010b). It is my tripartite analytical framework that will serve as the basis for the curricular and pedagogical applications offered in later sections of this book.

MEDIA LITERACY

Media literacy grew out of the field of communication studies in the second half of the 20th century. It was initially designed to challenge the dominant representations presented in the media, including stereotypical portrayals of race, gender, social class, age, and sexual orientation, and as a way of protecting children from the harmful effects of advertising, movies, and television (Hobbs & Jensen, 2009). Originally focused on advertising and television, this field of study is now concerned with the proliferation of digital media and its effects on society.

Media literacy has been defined as a body of knowledge or content to be acquired, a set of skills or competencies to be performed, or as a series of conceptual understandings to be learned (Buckingham, 2003). To bridge these diverse definitions, Meyrowitz (1998) postulated three different types of media literacy, namely:

1. media content literacy—how to access and analyze the messages in various media,
2. media grammar literacy—how various media are produced and constructed, and
3. medium literacy—how the medium shapes communication.

Each of Meyrowitz's components of media literacy focused on a different aspect of media literacy and suggested a different body of knowledge and set of competencies required by individuals in contemporary society.

In addition, Buckingham (2003) offered four key conceptual understandings that extend the scope of media literacy beyond the content and grammar of a medium itself to the production and dissemination of a whole range of contemporary and traditional media. His four key conceptual understandings focus on:

1. *Production*—the recognition that media are consciously manufactured, and that economic interests are at stake in media production.

2. *Language*—the understanding of how every medium has its own combinations of resources that it draws upon to communicate meanings. Each medium uses particular codes, conventions, or grammar in its construction.

3. *Representation*—the assertion that media offer a mediated version of the world, not the world itself. Each represents reality through the semiotic resources available, reflecting the interests and motivations of the creators.

4. *Audience*—the study of how audiences are targeted and measured, how media are disseminated, and how various constituencies use, interpret, analyze, and respond to various media.

Media literacy can also be defined as the ability to critically understand, question, and evaluate how media work to produce meanings, and how they organize, mediate, and construct reality. In other words, media literacy is concerned with how media impacts all aspects of our lives. The blending of critical perspectives with the cognitive thinking skills endorsed by early media literacy advocates moved the field forward, acknowledging both a social and pictorial turn (Mitchell, 1994). Parallel to turns across the social sciences, the shift from a focus on cognitive skills to social practices grounded media and visual literacy in sociocultural contexts and brought power relations, sites of production and reception, democratic principles, and identity into the discussion (Luke, 2000).

Media mediate the world rather than providing a transparent window through which to view the world (Buckingham, 2003). One of the basic premises of media literacy instruction is to support students as they examine media representations of the world in order to de-center these representational systems, or make the familiar strange enough to rethink how they are positioned by various media representations and how these representations affect one's life and society in general. Early definitions of media literacy suggested that media create messages that imposed meaning on an audience, reducing media literacy to a discussion of cognitive thinking skills. More contemporary definitions, however, include critical analysis of media and the mapping of subject positions in order to foreground the influence of diverse sociocultural contexts and perspectives.

As research and theories on media literacy evolve, the concept of *critical media literacy* has been taken up in earnest and is associated with critical theories and pedagogies in much the same way that critical literacy evolved from cognitive perspectives on literacy (Alvermann & Hagood, 2000; Street, 1995). To be critical, "assume[s] that humans are active agents whose reflective self-analysis and whose knowledge of the world leads to action that confronts old assumptions from the standpoint of new conditions" (Semali, 2000, p. 81). In addition, the meanings constructed by audiences of digital and print-based media are shaped by particular worldviews, positions, values, ideologies, and experiences.

The National Association of Media Literacy Educators (NAMLE), an organization dedicated to the conceptualization and application of media literacy education, is working to support the communication, creativity, collaboration, and critical thinking skills of children and young adults in relation to mass media, popular culture, and digital technologies (Hobbs & Jensen, 2009). The *Core Principles of Media Literacy Education in the United States*, adopted by the NAMLE board of directors in 2007, states, "the purpose of media literacy education is to help individuals of all ages develop the habits of inquiry and skills of expression they need to be critical thinkers, effective communicators, and active citizens in today's world" (NAMLE, 2007). An abbreviated version of their core principles is presented in Figure 2.3.

In addition to the core principles set forth by NAMLE, Hobbs (2011) offers five essential dimensions of digital and media literacy education. These essential dimensions outline a foundation for a media literacy curriculum and pedagogy. These essential dimensions are presented in Figure 2.4.

As educators working to bring principles of media literacy into the curriculum, it's important that the field of visual studies needs to move beyond cognitive perspectives of visual persuasion and analysis to include critical and sociocultural theories and perspectives. These theoretical tools will enable teachers and students to understand not only what messages are constructed, but how social, political, historical, and political contexts influence the production, dissemination, and reception of mass media. In much the same way as visual literacy needs to be incorporated into school curricula, media literacy is an important component of a comprehensive literacy framework.

MULTILITERACIES

The New London Group was brought together in 1994 to consider the state and future of literacy pedagogy and outlined an agenda for a *Pedagogy of Multiliteracies*. The published manifesto (New London Group, 1996) conceived "meaning-making as a form of design or active dynamic transformation of the social world" (Cope & Kalantzis, 2009, p. 193). The highly regarded members of this group addressed the increasingly multimodal nature of textual forms, and how these complex texts were integrated into everyday media and sociocultural practices.

The term *multiliteracies* or multiple literacies refers to the reconceptualization of literacy as a multidimensional set of competencies and social practices in response to the increasing complexity and multimodal nature of texts. Visual literacy, media literacy, critical literacy, computer literacy, and other types of literacies are brought together under this umbrella term to suggest the need to expand the concept of literacy beyond reading and writing print-based texts. As the texts that readers encounter grow in complexity, in both print and digital environments, the literacies required to navigate, interpret, design, and analyze these texts also grows

Figure 2.3. Media Literacy Education Core Principles from the NAMLE

1. Media Literacy Education requires active inquiry and critical thinking about the messages we receive and create.
2. Media Literacy Education expands the concept of literacy (i.e., reading and writing) to include all forms of media.
3. Media Literacy Education builds and reinforces skills for learners of all ages. As with print literacy, those skills necessitate integrated, interactive, and repeated practice.
4. Media Literacy Education develops informed, reflective, and engaged participants essential for a democratic society.
5.. Media Literacy Education recognizes that media are a part of culture and function as agents of socialization.
6. Media Literacy Education affirms that people use their individual skills, beliefs, and experiences to construct their own meanings from media messages.

Figure 2.4. Essential Dimensions of Media Literacy Education

1. *Access*—finding and sharing relevant information through a variety of media.
2. *Analyze*—using critical thinking to analyze message, purpose, target audience, quality, veracity, credibility, point of view, and potential consequences of media.
3. *Create*—generating content with awareness of purpose, audience, and composition techniques.
4. *Reflect*—considering the impact of media messages and technology tools upon thinking and actions in daily life, and applying social responsibility and ethical principles to our identity, communications and conduct.
5. *Act*—sharing knowledge and solving problems in variety of social settings, and participating as a member in various organizations and institutions in such settings.

in complexity. New technologies and a more global society require a rethinking of what it means to be literate in today's world. The skills required to be *proficient* in the past will no longer be sufficient by themselves as we continue into the new millennium.

CONCLUDING REMARKS

Chauvin (2003) proposed that definitions of visual literacy are debatable and used interchangeably, thus potentially creating confusion and disagreement within and across fields of study. While adding the term *multiliteracies* may only muddy the theoretical waters, it is important to define and distinguish the similarities and differences across these theoretical terrains to expand our conceptualization of visual literacies. The documented shift from a cognitive skills perspective to sociocultural and critical perspectives is an important aspect of visual, media, and multiliteracies. Expanding the theoretical perspectives teachers bring to the exploration of visual images, various digital and print-based media, and multimodal ensembles will help teachers as they support students literate development in the context of contemporary society.

3

Foundational Processes

Interpreting images is just that, interpretation, not the discovery of their truth.

—Gillian Rose (2001)

In this chapter, I discuss in greater detail the theories and concepts that serve as a foundation for the instructional approaches to be presented later in this book. Focusing on the processes humans use to interpret and analyze visual images and multimodal texts, this chapter will address the foundational processes of: (1) perception, (2) representation, (3) interpretation, and (4) ideology. Although these processes have been researched, discussed, theorized, and debated for centuries, it is important to have an understanding of the various perspectives and ideas that have been part of this evolution of ideas.

I have divided the chapter into two sections; the first section provides an overview of the four foundational processes mentioned previously, and the second section presents several well-known approaches or frameworks for interpreting visual images and multimodal ensembles. Together, these two sections will help teachers understand the various processes associated with making sense of visual images and multimodal ensembles and the theoretical tensions associated with this endeavor.

Debates concerning how ideas and meanings are represented, perceived, interpreted, and assigned ideological value will certainly continue long past the publication of this book. Barthes (1977b), O'Toole (1994), Hall (1997), Gombrich (1972), Arnheim (1986), and many others have offered their insights into how meanings and concepts are represented and how various interpretations are constructed and warranted. The expanding field of visual literacy combines psychological theories of perception with sociocultural and critical aspects of visual design, social semiotics, and cultural studies. Merging physiological and cognitive theories that focus on vision and perception with the social and cultural dimensions of visual literacies allows for a more inclusive and expansive approach for understanding multimodal ensembles and their impact on today's students.

The terminology used in this chapter may be new to some readers, while others may be familiar with particular terms but find they are used in ways specific to the ideas presented here. In the field of visual literacy, there is a great deal of over-lap in how some of these terms are used, and no single authoritative voice seems to be forthcoming. At times, variation in the use of these terms may be confusing, and other times it may be downright off-putting not to have consensus among theorists and fields of inquiry. However, the ambiguity across disciplines also pro-vides space for ideas to be reconsidered and reorganized in new and helpful ways.

Although the theories and concepts will be presented in distinct sections in this chapter, in the actual practice of reading and viewing a multimodal ensemble, these distinctions blur as each process interacts and influences the others during the production, reception, and distribution of various texts.

FOUNDATIONAL PROCESSES

Whether written language and visual images are capable of representing the same information in different forms, or different types of information in different ways is an area of debate within the multimodal and visual literacy community (Aiello, 2006; Hull & Nelson, 2005). In either case, written language and visual images work individually (within modes) and in concert (across modes) to convey mean-ing, share information, order our worlds, and develop our identities, both as indi-viduals and as a culture.

Language, in both written and oral form has been and continues to be, the primary way humans communicate with one another. Written language has domi-nated cultural and educational institutions for many centuries, allowing them to record and archive their existence. Print-based, written language is still viewed in Western cultures as the dominant and most valuable form of representation (Kress, 2004). Legal documents, the novel, and the college dissertation carry with them social capital and are valuable commercial and social texts.

As society moves away from the dominance of written language texts, we are also moving from the printed page to the electronic screen (Kress, 2010). Both of these changes, from language to image and from page to screen, represent fun-damental shifts in how we perceive the world and communicate meanings, and the modes and resources available for representing what we know. For example, in the late 1800s, the invention of the photographic process changed the way visual images were conceived of and reproduced. Until this period, visual images were often used as fine art or solely for purposes of entertainment rather than as evidence of actual events. Gradually, photographs took on the task of communi-cating evidence in news reports and legal disputes. As technologies for producing and distributing visual images emerged and expanded through television, movies, digital photography, and the Internet, they have challenged the cultural monopoly of written language (de Silva Joyce & Gaudin, 2007).

Beginning with cognitive and physiological theories of perception and con-tinuing through the processes of representation and interpretation, the following sections present a brief overview of these various concepts. These theories and processes are vital to understanding how multimodal ensembles work, the ways in which they can be interpreted, and their impact on the lives of the students in our classrooms.

PERCEPTION

Perception plays a central role in our understanding of the world. In our engagements with the world around us, our perceptual system, or what we call our *senses* allow us to gather information that helps us understand our experiences. Perception is a transaction between the qualities of the environments in which we live and the experiences a person brings to those qualities (Eisner, 2002). It is not simply the visual stimuli falling on one's retina, nor the physical sensations gathered through other senses that complete our perceptual process. The brain serves as a central interpreter, organizing and interpreting the data gathered through the senses, making sense of this information and acting according to its interpretations.

In the early 19th century, visual perception was considered the *passive stamping* done by exterior stimuli on the retina. However, neuroscientists have recently argued, "the brain is only interested in obtaining knowledge about those permanent, essential, or characteristic properties of objects and surfaces that allow it to categorize them" (Zeki, 1999, p. 77). Rather than conceptualizing perception as the passive impression of light on the retina, perception is considered an active process, where the brain selects from the myriad of stimuli available based on one's interests and knowledge. Perception is a dynamic process in which the brain automatically filters, discards, and selects information, and compares it to an individual's stored record (Stafford, 2008).

An important distinction to make is the difference between what Berger (1972) defined as *looking*, the physical act of light falling on the retina, and *seeing*, one's ability to transact with an image to construct meaning. Berger (1972) suggested that looking is a physiological or perceptual act, while seeing is an interpretive act based on sociocultural considerations and contexts. Looking or noticing requires *perceptivity*—one's ability to differentiate and experience relationships among qualities, in this context the components of multimodal ensembles (Eisner, 2002). It is our ability to discriminate among the various visual and textual elements presented in multimodal ensembles that influences our interpretive processes.

In addition, when we decide what to pay attention to, selecting particular aspects of our environment over others, we also decide what not to attend to. Our perceptual system simultaneously *limits* and *calls* attention to what we are able to perceive and understand. *Seeing* is an act of choice, through which viewers negotiate social relationships and meaning potentials, develop the social practice of interpreting, and learn how to navigate relationships of power in this process (Sturken & Cartwright, 2001).

In similar fashion to Berger, Rose (2001) distinguishes between *vision*, what the human eye is physiologically capable of seeing, and *visuality*, how vision is constructed. Seeing, unlike the registering of light on the retina or the physiological apprehension of sense data, is not unidirectional, innocent, or naive. It is guided by the experiences and knowledge of an individual transacting with a work of art or other aspect of one's environment. We attend to what we notice, and what we notice depends on what we understand.

Visual perception begins with attending to the visual stimuli presented, and interpretation is considered a secondary contemplation or analysis of the stimuli attended to. However, this distinction is never absolute, since what we see is affected by what we know. Gombrich (1961) asserted, "the innocent eye is blind" (p. 298). Goodman (1976) insisted, "the eye comes always ancient to its work, not only how, but what it sees is regulated by need and prejudice" (p. 72). In addition, Graham (1990) argues, "readers' heads are not empty of pictures when they open a picture book, any more than their heads are empty of language when they open a text" (p. 18). Beardsley (1981) suggested, "a picture is two things at once: it is a design, and it is a picture *of* something. In other words, it presents something to the eye for direct inspection, and it represents something that exists, or might exist outside the picture frame" (p. 267).

Visual images, like words in a text, have meaning because students bring meaning and experiences to them. We cannot interpret aspects of our environment that we have not perceived, and what is perceived can change based on what we already know and have experienced.

Our experiences and perceptual apparatus serve as lenses through which we experience the world. "We see through the frameworks and filters produced by our culture and by our personal histories" (Schirato & Webb, 2004, p. 1). Perception and interpretation are not separate mental operations, but rather thoroughly interconnected social processes, and any approach to understanding visual images or multimodal texts must acknowledge this interconnection (Serafini, 2010b).

These assertions concerning perception have important implications for the instructional experiences we offer students. As teachers, we need to pay attention to what students are attending to, and what they are ignoring when they transact with multimodal ensembles. Since the perceptual and interpretive processes are inextricably linked, we cannot expect students to understand that which they do not notice. We need to help students pay attention to the various structures, elements, and compositions of multimodal ensembles in order to interpret what they experience.

REPRESENTATION

In addition to written language, photography, painting, architecture, and sculpture are all representational or *semiotic* systems used to communicate meaning.

Semiotics is a branch of philosophy that focuses on signs and how we interpret the various signs we encounter. A *sign* is something that stands for something else, in some capacity, for some particular person. Written language, photographs, street signs, paintings, and diagrams are all signs in that they represent ideas and concepts in some capacity for some groups of people.

For example, written language is a representational system that connects *signifiers* (words and letters) with *signifieds* (ideas, things, and concepts). A sign brings together the signifier or *sign vehicle* and what is to be signified (Saussure, 1910). The words (signifiers) *dog, chien,* and *perro* all refer to the furry animal (object or concept) many people own that barks and chases cats. The words that refer to these objects or concepts may be different, but they refer in general to the thing we have come to know as a dog. None of these words or signifiers for dog is inherently better than any other, but within the language or system of representation in which they are used, they each become relevant and are conventionalized within a particular culture.

When we read the word *dog*, there is no specific dog we all think of. Rather, it is the concept of "dogness" that each person interprets in slightly or drastically different ways. One person may love dogs, while others are afraid of them. The signs we use do not create stable or direct relationships between signifiers and signifieds. Rather, people construct relationships between words and objects for themselves every time they transact with signs in their environment. There is no universal, stable meaning for any sign, although some meanings become conventionalized and are more widely accepted than others.

Representation has been described as a process of "transforming the contents of consciousness within the constraints and affordances of a material" (Eisner, 2002, p. 6). Representation stabilizes an idea or concept in a durable, public, and primarily visible form. In addition, systems of representation organize, construct, and mediate our understandings of the world (Sturken & Cartwright, 2001). In other words, representation requires the *realization* of meaning in a particular form. Realization is the process of selecting from and transforming existing resources given the intentions of its rhetor and the limitations and affordances of a particular mode. It is a sociocultural process of realizing meanings in particular semiotic forms.

Meanings precede the act of representation or their realization in material form. Eisner (2002) reminds us that realizing meanings is not a linear or unidirectional process, in which the rhetor inscribes meanings directly into a representational form for the reader to decode. He suggests it is more like a conversation with emerging possibilities or a variety of meaning potentials from which the reader or viewer transacts. In addition, representational and interpretational processes are always mediated by the materiality and affordances of the mode in which they are realized.

Representations may be categorized as *mimetic*—representations that resemble or *mimic* the things they represent, for example photographs, or as *constructionist*—symbolic or metaphorical connections between objects and concepts and their representations (Hall, 1997). Mimetic representations resemble visually what they are representing, while constructionist representations are conventionalized through their use in social contexts. Pierce (1960) categorized types of representations or *signs* as:

1. *icons*—representations that are based on resemblance (i.e., photographs or realistic portraits),
2. *indices*—representations that refer or indicate something else (i.e., arrows or footprints), and
3. *symbols*—arbitrary representations based on social conventions (i.e., words or numbers).

No matter how these representations are categorized, resources are used to represent meanings in some physical or conceptual form for others to interpret.

In general, not all representations or signs work in the same way to represent objects, concepts, and meanings. The most important consideration is that there is no unmediated association between the actual world or reality and the representations people construct; rather, sociocultural and individual experiences influence the representations constructed and the meanings associated with these representations. Culture, experiences, and ideology always influence our ways of interpreting and representing the world. A drawing of a dog is not an actual dog and only represents it in particular ways through particular semiotic resources.

A further distinction is offered by Kress (2010), where he distinguishes between *representation*, which is focused on the needs, interests, and expectations of the rhetor giving material form through socially available semiotic resources, and *communication*, which is a social activity focused on the interactions of the rhetor and others, and the needs, interests, and histories of the audience. This distinction focuses on the motivation of the rhetor on one hand, and the needs and interests of the audience on the other. Both of these sites of representation—the production and reception of a work of art, as well as the site of the work of art itself—are important considerations in the interpretive process (Rose, 2001).

Visual images represent a different relationship between an actual object and its sign than written language does. Whereas the word *dog* does not look like a dog, a realistic painting or photograph of a dog may closely resemble a dog. Yet, we must remember that a photograph is still a form of representation no matter how close the resemblance. A photograph of the Empire State Building is not the Empire State Building that was erected in New York City many years ago. Magritte's famous painting the *Treachery of Images,* which featured a painting of a smoking pipe and the caption in French, "*Ceci n'est pas une pipe*" (This is not a pipe) reminds us that representations are not the things in and of themselves. Words and images represent our worlds differently, draw upon distinct logics (temporal and spatial), and are both mediated by the sociocultural contexts in which they are produced and received.

Systems of representations are not simply innocent means of communication, but have been produced in the course of cultural histories stemming from specific interests and purposes. Systems of representation offer *meaning potentials* or fields of possible meanings that are activated by producers and consumers of visual images and multimodal texts in the act of interpretation (Aiello, 2006). Particular or dominant meanings are naturalized through constant associations with particular perceived objects. A red rose has come to be symbol of erotic love in Western cultures, not through some resemblance to love itself, but through continued association with this concept. This process of realization of meaning potentials, also known as *signification*, is a socially contextualized practice. In other words, meaning potentials are realized in particular contexts through repeated use (Scollon & Scollon, 2003).

How we represent ideas and concepts, and the modes through which we allow our students to represent theirs has important implications for classroom instruction. Written language dominated literacy instruction for the better part of the 20th century, yet other modes have been made available and access to digital modes of representation are increasing. Written language is not as effective a mode as photography or a drawing for conveying spatial relations and physical characteristics, and single photographs are not as good at revealing processes that take place over time as video recordings. New modes of representation need to be brought into the classroom, providing students a wider range of options and resources for sharing what they know and have learned.

INTERPRETATION

Interpretation is the process of making sense of the world around us. It is what we do every day to understand ourselves, our interactions with others, and the contexts in which we live. For purposes of this chapter, I will focus on interpretation as a process for making sense of the visual images, written language, and design features of multimodal ensembles.

What a visual image or multimodal ensemble means depends upon one's past experiences and knowledge, as well as the intentions of the artist, the contexts of reception and production, and the work of art itself. Theories of interpretation must take into account the written text, visual image, or multimodal ensemble under consideration; the knowledge and perspectives of the student, the context of reception, and the context of the production of the work itself.

To begin, all interpretations are constructed. The world itself may not require a person's consciousness to exist, but images of that world and interpretations of said images clearly do (Mitchell, 1986). In other words, our senses, minds, and bodies always mediate our understandings of the external world; we have no access to the world as it is in and of itself. Systems of representation mediate between the world and our experiences, and these representations influence how we come to understand it. In other words, reality has a separate existence from our perceptions, representations, and interpretations of it.

The process of representation, like the process of interpretation, is not disinterested. All systems of representation reflect historical, political, and social contexts and power relations, which serve to conceal the historical character and class bias of that system under a façade of naturalness and universality (Marx, 1930). These sociocultural forces inform and intersect all representational systems and interpretive processes. In addition, culture and ideology influence the interpretive process. Stable universal meanings are not fixed within a visual image or textual representation. Rather, representations offer a set of meaning potentials with which students transact and construct meanings (Aiello, 2006). Because these meanings are not fixed, nor stable, they give agency to the student, who can then revise and renegotiate meanings with others.

Rose (2001) posits three *sites* at which interpretations are constructed: (1) the production of a visual image, (2) the visual image itself, and (3) the reception of the visual image by an audience (p. 16). In order to critically approach visual images and multimodal texts, Rose (2001) suggests that we take images seriously, think about the social conditions and effects of visual objects, and consider our own way of looking at images. In her review of visual methodologies, she expands the interpretive process beyond a cognitive, individual perspective to include the sociocultural contexts and influences on the production, reception and distribution of visual images and multimodal ensembles.

Every act of representation and interpretation involves the following four dimensions: (1) viewer—the person transacting with the visual image, (2) rhetor or designer—the creator of the visual image, (3) multimodal ensemble—the visual image itself, and (4) immediate-sociocultural contexts—where the image is viewed. Each of these dimensions represents a theoretical dimension from which interpretive processes and theories have been constructed. Some theories focus more on the viewer and the point of reception, while others focus on the work of art itself, or the contexts of its production, while still others focus on how sociocultural influences impact the interpretive processes of the viewer.

During the act of interpreting, viewers fix meanings using the codes and conventions available in their sociocultural contexts (Hall, 1997). These meanings are not stable, nor permanent; they are open to revision and negotiation as they are shared with other reader-viewers. The rhetor, or designer, may intend specific meanings, but does not have, as Barthes (1977a) declared in "The Death of the Author," a privileged position from which to assert which meanings are true or correct. Multimodal ensembles and visual images contain structures and visual features that need to be considered in the act of interpretation and all of this takes place and is influenced by the immediate sociocultural contexts of the process of interpretation. Various theories highlight different dimensions in this process, but all must include to some degree each of these dimensions.

In contemporary theories of interpretation, the interpretive process begins with a literal or denotative level of meaning based on perception of visual and textual elements (attention to the physical effects of visual stimuli on the retina), and progresses through various structural perspectives, where viewers construct meaning in transaction with written texts and visual images, culminating in a critical or sociocultural frame of analysis (Serafini, 2010b). To expand the foundation of the interpretive process to address both the role of the individual and cultural contexts in the interpretive process, I offer several assertions based on sociocultural and post-structural theories of reading and literary comprehension (see Figure 3.1).

Based on these assertions, meanings constructed during the act of interpretation are socially embedded, temporary, partial, and plural. There is not a single, objective truth about a particular multimodal text or visual image, but many truths, each with its own authority and its own warrants for viability aligned with particular interpretive theories and perspectives (Aiello, 2006; Elkins, 2008). The meanings constructed by students at any one point in time are plural or *polysemous*, and open for reconsideration when transacting with a visual image or multimodal ensemble.

Students construct interpretations, not as originators of meaning, but as human subjects positioned through social, political, and historical practices that remain the location of a constant struggle over power. We cannot know objects in reality in and of themselves; we always are bound by our senses and interpretive contexts. Nor can we represent the meanings we want neutrally, objectively, or in their entirety. In other words, we cannot step outside our senses, minds, and cultures to know something from a "god's eye view" or fully objective perspective.

Figure 3.1. Post-Structural Assertions Concerning the Interpretive Process

1. All texts, including multimodal ensembles, are social artifacts created by rhetors and interpreted by viewers that are embedded in particular social contexts and practices.
2. Interpretations are always socially constructed and embedded in historical, political, and social contexts.
3. Interpretations are always political, working toward particular interests and groups of people.
4. Every interpretation has particular cultural capital; some are more privileged than others in particular contexts, for example classroom settings.
5. There is no unmediated access to texts; there are only particular interpretations that are privileged over other interpretations. In other words, there is no transcendent authority available as an objective interpretation from which to compare other interpretations.

In summary, viewers interpret visual images and multimodal ensembles in specific sociocultural contexts based on their personal and cultural histories. We are bound by our senses and experiences to be able to only offer our own subjective interpretations. We may privilege certain interpretations over others, but there is no transcendent authority available to ascertain which interpretations are correct and which ones are faulty.

The process of privileging particular interpretations over others has important implications as we begin to consider various instructional approaches, and how we decide which interpretations of visual images and multimodal texts to endorse. In classrooms, we must open up spaces for our students' interpretations to be considered, negotiated, and revised. Instructional approaches for interpreting multimodal ensembles should reveal the conventions of visual meaning and make these available for negotiation and revision. Our discussions have to allow for possibilities, rather than reducing individual ideas to consensual, mainstream agreements. The meaning of a picture does not declare itself by a simple and direct reference to the objects it depicts; viewers must learn the processes and structures through which images speak (Mitchell, 1994).

IDEOLOGY

Aiello (2006) defines ideology as "a set of socially constructed meanings or norms that become embedded and naturalized in the cultural fabric, to the extent that they become invisible or common sense" (p. 92). As we are confronted with particular ideas and concepts, they become part of our mainstream cultural heritage, and these ways of seeing influence our understandings in ways that aren't readily apparent.

Innocent and unbiased museum curators do not create innocent and objective exhibits that can be assessed by innocent and unbiased viewers who construct objective interpretations of what they experience. Rather, students with unique histories and prior experiences are confronted by fine art, picturebooks, and visual images in specific immediate and sociocultural contexts. In addition, works of art are created by authors and artists with unique sociocultural and political histories, selected by gallery owners, graphic designers, publishers, museum curators, and advertising executives to serve specific needs and interests. In each of these instances, ideology plays a role in the interpretations constructed and the meanings endorsed and privileged by specific groups.

Hall (1997) asserts, "interpretation is a mental process of acceptance and rejection of meanings and associations that adhere to a given image through the force of dominant ideologies" (p. 57). For Hall (1997), there are three types of interpretations that are available to viewers:

1. *Dominant*—where the dominant message is received in an unquestioning stance.
2. *Negotiated*—where meanings are questioned and negotiated.
3. *Oppositional*—where there is disagreement or rejection of the dominant message.

Dominant meanings or interpretations are socially agreed upon meanings that emerge out of social relations, and gain power in the contexts of their creation and dissemination. The fields of cultural and visual studies focus on revealing how particular interpretations and cultural norms become embedded in media messages and visual images in ways that allow them to be reinforced and internalized, thereby becoming dominant. For example, the interpretations constructed by prominent professors of art history and notable art critics are privileged by society due to their creators' education, experiences, and social status, not because of these experts' ability to ascertain the one true meaning of a work. Interpretations offered by experienced and notable critics should help students understand the potential meanings of a visual image, the various influences on their interpretations, and the contexts of the construction of these interpretations. Critics' interpretations should not be viewed as universal truths to be memorized; rather their offerings should be viewed as the art of saying useful things about subtle and complex objects and events so that less sophisticated viewers can see and understand what they did not see and understand before (Eisner, 1998).

An important aspect of ideology is that the fixing of meanings may be contested or unfixed since these meanings are historically or culturally constructed. Iedema (2001) suggests that being able to critically analyze texts "provides the possibility for renegotiating the meanings inherent in such constructs rather than seeing these as fixed, irrevocable, and natural" (p. 201). As much as ideology plays a role in the construction of particular interpretations, it also creates a space where any and all interpretations can be called into question, challenged, and negotiated. Our instructional practices should open up spaces for the reconsideration of the potential meanings of a work of art or multimodal ensemble, not close down the discussion. We need to embrace both the dominant and oppositional interpretations of an image or text if we are to open up space for our students to interpret these entities for themselves. We also need to help students understand that all interpretations are social constructions and how the sociocultural contexts in which they live affect their interpretive processes.

In summary, the processes of perceiving, representing, and interpreting a visual image or multimodal ensemble always occur within the ideological and sociocultural contexts in which they operate. As viewers of visual images and multimodal ensembles, students perceive particular aspects of these entities, consider how things are represented, construct interpretations to be shared, and negotiate and revise their interpretations in the context of classroom experiences and discussions. The revising and renegotiation of meanings associated with visual images and multimodal ensembles provides a space for countering dominant ideologies and meanings, enhancing the agency of the student, and giving power to previously disenfranchised groups.

FRAMEWORKS FOR INTERPRETING VISUAL IMAGES AND MULTIMODAL ENSEMBLES

In the past, art historians and theorists have created various procedures for ensuring valid interpretations of works of art. Trying to create a more objective process for interpreting fine art, Feldman (1981) suggested there are four steps for interpreting a work of art: (1) naming and describing the facts or literal aspects of the work, (2) analyzing the facts and building visual evidence, (3) interpreting the evidence, and (4) judging the work of art and estimating its value as art. In addition, Feldman (1981) offered the following characteristics of a quality interpretation of a work of art:

1. *Completeness*—most of the facts have been explained.
2. *Persuasiveness*—the argument is logical and feels convincing.
3. *Personal Relevance*—appeals to viewers' knowledge.
4. *Durability*—makes sense over time.
5. *Intellectual Force*—valid connections between the work of art and the world of ideas.
6. *Insight*—explains why a work is or is not enjoyable to the viewer.
7. *Originality*—the interpretation discovers fresh meanings in the work as it relates to the world and the life of the viewer.

This approach has been defined as *compositional interpretation* or the "good eye" theory (Rose, 2001). Functioning as a type of *visual connoisseurship*, this interpretive process considers contextual information about the production of a work of art, the artist, and the composition of the work of art itself. This process suggests one can objectively look at a work of art and judge it on its own terms, or look at images just for what they are, rather than for what they do or how they were used (Rose, 2001). This interpretive process also assumes that images live in a vacuum and critics can step outside of their own biases and contexts to render objective interpretations about the images they critique. Simply judging the provenance, composition, color, logic of configuration, and expressive content of an image or multimodal ensemble without regard for the contexts of its production and reception narrows our interpretations of any work of art.

The good eye theory does not take into account the sociocultural, historical, and political nature of the interpretive process. As becomes clear as we progress through these various frameworks, the quest for an objective interpretation becomes problematic. All interpretations are situated in specific social, historical, and political contexts, and are subjected to the knowledge and experiences of the person or group doing the interpreting. While Feldman's characteristics addressed the role of the art historian and the work of art in the interpretive process, for many theorists, he did not go far enough to include the sociocultural, historical, and political contexts in which interpretations are constructed and offered. Recently, visual culture and art theorists have abandoned trying to identify a stable foundation for an objective interpretation of a work of art as they acknowledge the role of the individual and one's sociocultural contexts and influences in the interpretive process (van Leeuwen & Jewitt, 2001).

Based on a semiotic perspective, Barthes (1977b) distinguishes between the *denotation* and *connotation* of an image or multimodal ensemble. Barthes (1977b) suggests that the viewer of an image receives its literal or descriptive meanings or message (denotation), and the cultural meanings or message (connotations) simultaneously. The literal meaning is based on initial perception of what is actually in the image, and the connotations are those meanings that the viewer brings to the image, both *personally* and *culturally*.

Iconography is a branch of the visual arts concerned with interpreting the themes inherent in visual arts and its associated meanings and content (van Straten, 1994). Panofsky's (1955) model of interpretation began with constructing *pre-iconographic* descriptions, *the recognition of pure forms*, defined as direct association of a new visual experience with one's memory and knowledge (Hasenmueller, 1987). The *iconographic* process is an interpretation of secondary or conventional subject matter, themes, and concepts. The identification of such images, themes, and concepts, in contrast to identifying forms, distinguished the iconographic level from the pre-iconographic level. For example, if a person walks down the street and raises her hand as she passes by another person, the act is initially perceived as a physical motion, but can also be interpreted as a form of social etiquette.

Taking the interpretive process a step further, *iconological* processes focused on ascertaining the underlying principles of a nation, culture, or period that was rendered through a work of art. Iconology can be viewed as an ideological interpretation of an image or work of art. Panofsky

> . . . knew the difficulties of verifying the conclusions of investigation that transcended empirical data, however, progressing through the identification of forms, the construction of images and themes, to the interpretation of these images in light of the sociocultural contexts of these images was the basis of his interpretive framework. (Hasenmueller, 1987, p. 291)

Panofsky provided a framework for acknowledging the literal details of an image while including interpretive processes that involved social, historical, and cultural dimensions.

O'Toole (1994) suggests there are four ways of understanding and analyzing works of art and other visual forms: (1) a historical approach centered on the circumstance of the work's commission, (2) an iconographical approach that emphasizes the origins of the work's subject matter through literary or philosophical sources, (3) a textual approach that focuses on a study of the pure composition of the work, and (4), a semiotic approach, focuses on the representational, interpersonal and compositional metafunctions first set forth by Halliday (1978). The first three approaches were considered traditional approaches while the fourth or semiotic approach, which he outlined in great detail for interpreting painting, sculpture, and architecture, encompasses the three traditional approaches and goes further to offer a more complete and synthesized interpretation of the works under study. It is O'Toole's semiotic approach that aligns with current approaches and provides a starting point for the construction of my own analytical framework.

Rose (2001) distinguished three dimensions that can contribute to a critical understanding of visual images, namely, (1) technological—any form or apparatus designed to be looked at or enhance natural vision, for example painting, television, or the Internet, (2) compositional—formal structures or strategies, for example color, spatial organization, or content, and (3) social—the range of economic, social, and political relations, institutions, and practices that surround an image, for example art galleries, schools, or cultural groups (pp. 16–17). Rose (2001) noted that some methodologies concentrated on the image itself, focusing on how composition, color, spatial organization, and light contribute to an image's *expressive content* or the combined effect of visual form and subject matter. Although Rose (2001) acknowledged that visual images do not exist in a vacuum, and looking at them for what they are in themselves neglects the ways in which visual images are produced and interpreted through particular social practices, viewers still needed to consider what was presented or rendered in an image, and the structures and modalities that were used in creating images before proceeding to an ideological analysis.

Considering the extensive work that has gone before me, and working across various approaches for interpreting multimodal texts, I have developed a tripartite framework that addresses the perceptual, structural, and ideological dimensions of interpretation (Serafini, 2010b). In Figure 3.2, I present an overview of this framework. Each of the dimensions is nested within the other to connote the interrelationships among the dimensions.

This framework is offered as a composite of the interpretive approaches to visual images and multimodal texts reviewed previously and available in the research and theoretical literature. Supporting students as they approach, navigate, and analyze visual images and multimodal ensembles is an important part of literacy education; and providing them with the vocabulary necessary for discussing these various dimensions or perspectives is a good first step in students' visual literacy development.

Figure 3.2. Perceptual, Structural, and Ideological Interpretive Dimensions

1. Perceptual—Noticing, Navigating, and Naming Elements of Visual Images and Multimodal Texts

   - Focus on What Is Presented in the Image Itself
   - Noticing Visual Elements and Composition
   - Perceived Through the Sense of Sight (Good Eye)
   - Inventory of Contents
   - Navigating and Naming Visual Elements
   - Basic Elements of Design—Line, Shape, Pattern
   - Denotation

2. Structural—Grammar, Structures, and Conventions of Visual Images and Multimodal Texts

   - Codes and Conventions of Visual Elements
   - Analysis of Visual Grammar and Designs
   - Draws on Semiotic Theories of Meaning
   - Looking for Meanings, Themes, Messages
   - Symbols and Recurring Patterns (Motifs)
   - Connotation

3. Ideological—Analysis of the Social Practices and Sociocultural Contexts of Visual Images and Multimodal Texts

   - Considering the Context, Culture, and History of an Image
   - Social Meanings of the Actors and Events Portrayed
   - Text and Image as Social Artifact
   - Sites of Production and Reception
   - Myths, Cultural Symbols, and Messages
   - Social Semiotic Theories of Meaning

CONCLUDING REMARKS

In summary, the approaches presented above draw from different fields of inquiry and offer a variety of analytical perspectives for looking at visual images, art, and multimodal texts. Each approach comes to the act of interpretation with different theoretical assumptions and analytical tools. Each theorist acknowledges the need to perceive what is rendered or presented in an image or text before interpreting what is depicted, and to further consider the social, cultural, political, and historical contexts of the reception and production of these texts and images. Theories of visual literacies have progressed from a cognitive perspective on developing a critical eye in individual viewers to understanding the sociocultural, historical, and contextual dimensions of making sense of visual images.

The processes of representation (how meanings are realized) and interpretation (how meanings are constructed) have perceptual, cognitive, social, and ideological dimensions that must be considered as educators begin to design curricular and pedagogical frameworks. Mitchell (1994) suggested the meaning of a picture does not declare itself by a simple and direct reference to the objects it depicts—students must learn how *images speak*. As educators, we need to provide strategies and analytical procedures for our students to be able approach, navigate, interpret, and discuss the various visual images and multimodal ensembles they encounter in their everyday lives.

Attending to the perceptual qualities of a multimodal ensemble is just as important as considering the ideological and sociocultural contexts in which they are viewed. The theoretical framework presented in this chapter allows us to address the perceptual, structural, and ideological aspects of visual images and multimodal ensembles in order to teach students how to interpret them.

4

Understanding Multimodality

Central assumptions of multimodal approaches to representation and communication are: (a) that communication is always and inevitably multimodal; and (b) that each of the modes available for representation in a culture provides specific potentials and limitations for communication.

—Kress and van Leeuwen (1996)

For many years the research on representation and discourse has focused on language to the exclusion of other modes or modalities. Stockl (2007) writes, "the dominance of linguistics, however, and the concentration on language as the central mode, paired with a lack of adequate models for the analysis of other modes, made verbal mono-modality appear to be the standard and dominant form of communication" (p. 10). This focus on language as the dominant mode of communication has overshadowed research in multimodality until recently.

MULTIMODALITY

More than simply asking what modes or multimodal ensembles *are*, we need to be asking what multimodal ensembles *do*. An important aspect of the multimodal nature of contemporary visual sites is not simply how discrete sign systems or individual modes articulate and represent meaning potentials, but how meaning is constructed as these sign systems interact with one another (O'Halloran, 2004). Representing and interpreting multimodal ensembles means not only acknowledging the integration of visual images with other modes of representation and communication, but understanding how these socially constructed ensembles are integrated into cultural life (Sturken & Cartwright, 2001).

Multiple modes are used in a variety of settings for a range of social purposes. The use of one mode or another is "guided by socially determined intentions and realizes group interests, subjective points of view or ideological stances" (Stockl, 2007, p. 10). In other words, the sociocultural dimensions of various modes are as important in understanding multimodal ensembles and multimodality as their technological and material dimensions.

One framework for considering what multimodal texts do is based on the work of Halliday (1978), who proposed a classification of three metafunctions (see Figure 4.1) for written and spoken language that has been taken up by theorists working with multimodal ensembles (Kress & van Leeuwen, 1996; Machin, 2007; O'Halloran, 2004; O'Toole, 1994). Halliday's (1978) work, commonly referred to as *systemic functional linguistics*, included three metafunctions, namely:

1. *the ideational metafunction*—how language is used to represent ideas and concepts,
2. *the interpersonal metafunction*—how language establishes relationships between producer and receiver, and
3. *the textual metafunction*—how language is organized in particular ways.

These three metafunctions provide "a conceptual framework for representing the social context as the semiotic environment in which people exchange meanings" (Halliday, 1978, p. 110). Halliday's metafunctions are aspects of language that make it possible for communicating across time and contexts. Various theorists and educators have reconceptualized Halliday's three metafunctions as a foundation for considering multimodal ensembles (Aiello, 2006; Iedema, 2003; O'Toole, 1994). From these various reconceptualizations, I have decided to use the terms (1) *representational*, (2) *interpersonal*, and (3) *compositional* metafunctions as composites to reflect the multimodal nature of the texts to which these metafunctions are referring (see Figure 4.1).

The *representational metafunction* refers to the content or potential ideas, stories, and concepts represented in a multimodal ensemble. For example, mathematical symbols represent certain numbers or concepts. The *interpersonal metafunction* refers to the relationship created between the actors or objects in an image and how they are perceived by the viewer, for example whether people in an image are looking directly at the viewer or away from him. The *compositional metafunction* refers to the spatial organization of elements and the framing devices that connect and separate these elements in multimodal ensembles. An example of the compositional metafunction would be the use of borders or space in an image to separate individual features. Drawing on these three metafunctions, theorists and educators are better able to understand how the various features of multimodal

Figure 4.1. Multimodal Metafunctions

1. *Representational metafunction*—a variety of semiotic resources and modalities are used to articulate and represent ideas and concepts.
2. *Interpersonal metafunction*—a variety of semiotic resources and modalities are used to establish relationships between the producer (artist or writer) and the consumer (reader or viewer).
3. *Compositional metafunction*—a variety of semiotic resources and modalities are used in the organization of multimodal elements.

ensembles work to offer meaning potentials and the visual and verbal cues students may draw upon to interpret them.

SOCIOCULTURAL DIMENSIONS OF MULTIMODALITY

To extend the discussion of modes and modality from a material or technological perspective to a sociocultural one, modes need to be reconceptualized as cultural resources for the articulation, representation, interpretation, and communication of concepts and information. The technologies of representation and those of communication and dissemination are everywhere bound up with social and ethical values, and cannot be theorized on the basis of materiality alone (Kress, 2003).

Lankshear and Knobel (2006) have coined the terms *new technical stuff* and *new ethos stuff* to refer to the differences between the material or technological aspects and the sociocultural aspects of new literacies. The evolutionary trajectories of multimodality and new literacies go beyond the technical aspects of digital environments and hypertexts to incorporate new ways of participating and collaborating in social environments. For example, Wikipedia has not only changed how we look up information, it has changed who has the authority to control which definitions and information are made available, forever blurring the line between informer and informed. The incorporation of various modes in a multimodal ensemble and new ways of disseminating these texts is more than an evolution in technology; it is also a change in the social, political, and cultural dimensions of what it means to be fully literate.

Changes in communicative environments suggest that social practices related to multimodality and literacy are being reshaped as advances in technology provide new social environments and possibilities for producers and interpreters of multimodal texts (Bearne, 2003). As digital technologies make producing and disseminating multimodal ensembles easier, changes in the way people use these texts and the power relations between producer and consumer are continually evolving; the nature of authorship, reader, viewer, and publisher have begun to blur as changes in the sociocultural practices involving the production, dissemination, and interpretation of multimodal ensembles occur.

A good example of these changes can be seen in the evolution of online publishing. At first, the electronic version of a text (e-book) was viewed as simply a new delivery mechanism, offering readers an alternative to buying paper versions of novels. However, the changes that have occurred as a result of this technology have had both social and commercial ramifications. For better or worse, brick and mortar bookstores have gone out of business because of these changes in the delivery of texts. E-readers have not only made transportation of multiple texts easier, they have also provided avenues for readers to share highlights and commentaries with other readers across time and space. These technological changes have produced social and economic shifts in how our society reads and shares texts.

RESEARCH ON MULTIMODALITY

Multimodality has been conceptualized as a theory of communication, a field of inquiry, a perspective on texts, and as a research methodology. A wide variety of theoretical perspectives have been used to inform theories of multimodality and approaches for interpreting visual images and multimodal ensembles. Some of the areas of inquiry include: (1) Visual Literacy, (2) Iconography and Iconology, (3) Media Studies, (4) Visual Discourse Analysis, (5) Cultural Studies, (6) Art History, and (7) Qualitative Content Analysis.

The research on multimodality and multimodal ensembles has greatly expanded in recent years. Drawing primarily on systemic functional linguistics and social semiotics, research on multimodal texts and multimodality focuses on three perspectives or areas of inquiry: social semiotics, multimodal discourse analysis, and multimodal interaction analysis (Jewitt, 2009). Figure 4.2 provides a quick overview of these perspectives and resources for extending reading.

Each of the approaches to multimodal research draws heavily on the semiotic theories of Saussure (1910), Barthes (1977b), and Pierce (1960), as well as Halliday's (1978) systemic functional linguistics. The various approaches differ in their historical influences, treatment of the social aspects of semiotic theories, emphasis on the context of the design and interpretation of multimodal texts, and the influence or agency of the producer. A more detailed analysis of these approaches is beyond the scope of this book. However, the theoretical foundation supporting the three research agendas listed below informs the perspectives and pedagogical approaches presented throughout this book (see Figure 4.2). For more information, Jewitt's (2009) *Routledge Handbook of Multimodal Analysis* is an important resource.

ESSENTIAL ASPECTS OF MULTIMODALITY

In this section, I will discuss four essential aspects of multimodality: (1) Materiality, (2) Modal Fixing and Aptness, (3) Affordances and Limitations, and (4) Design. Each aspect of multimodality plays an important role in understanding how multimodal ensembles are constructed and organized, how various representational systems are used, and how these images and texts work in particular social contexts.

Materiality

In addition to the different social practices and semiotic resources associated with various modes, modes have different physical aspects or *materiality*. Every mode is realized and constructed in different materials, for example clay, stone, paint, sound waves, digital pixels, wood, paper, or canvas. Because various modes

Figure 4.2. Areas of Research on Multimodality

1. *Social Semiotics* (usually associated with the work of Kress & van Leeuwen, 1996)—drawing on the work of Saussure in semiotics, and expanding the social approach to linguistics by Halliday (1978), social semiotics looks to understand multimodal texts as complex signs used in the realization, articulation, and interpretation of meanings. This approach focuses on how the context of communication and the interests and needs of the sign maker shaped the meaning potentials of multimodal texts.
2. *Multimodal Discourse Analysis* (usually associated with the work of Baldry & Thibault, 2006, and O'Halloran, 2004)—drawing extensively on Halliday's systemic functional linguistics, this approach focuses on discourse and how it is realized in multimodal ensembles and social contexts. Building on O'Toole's visual analysis of sculpture, painting, and architecture (O'Toole, 1994), multimodal discourse analysis emphasizes Halliday's metafunctions, and how various semiotic resources are used and combined in a variety of multimodal ensembles.
3. *Multimodal Interaction Analysis* (usually associated with the work of Norris, 2004, and Scollon & Scollon, 2003)—multimodal interaction analysis focuses on the physical and material aspects of language and how it is situated and realized in social contexts. It emphasizes the notions of context and situated interaction and the actions taken by social actors through multimodal meditational means.

Source: Adapted from Jewitt, 2009.

have different material aspects, they realize meanings in different ways. Electronic images are dynamic in nature, capable of being easily manipulated through computer software, whereas printed images are more permanent and require more work to alter once they have been produced in printed forms.

The differences in the materials used to realize and represent the rhetor's intended meanings influences what meaning potentials are communicated. Marble sculpture represents ideas and concepts differently than written language does. All meanings cannot be realized in every material, and designers select from various modes and their associated materials to *fix* certain meaning potentials in their creations. Once fixed in a particular material, they can be shared and used as a means of communication.

An example may be helpful before proceeding further. Oral language is fixed through sound waves and draws upon the semiotic resources of volume, intonation, phrasing, tone, and rate in the process of communication. Our talk is often accompanied by facial and hand gestures. The material aspects of oral language are not permanent unless captured using an audio- or video-recording device. Written language, however, has different material aspects. Meanings are realized through a particular script or typography, rendered on paper or in digital form, which makes it easy to distribute through electronic media across great distances. Tangible artifacts like books and posters can be archived and made available for future generations, but must be physically transported to other places. When we add visual images, design elements, sound effects, and music to written or oral language in digital formats we simply expand the potential for expressing and communicating our meanings and messages.

Modal Fixing and Aptness

Particular meanings, or what Eisner (2002) refers to as *contents of consciousness*, are selected by the rhetor to be represented in the various modes and resources available. Meanings are fixed or punctuated at a certain time and place within a particular representational system, given the affordances and limitations of the selected modes and materials. For example, we might choose to write a note to ourselves at a given time to remind us of something we want to remember later. At that moment, our meanings and intentions are fixed in this particular mode of representation using the materials available, possibly a pencil and a scrap of paper. It is the material realization of our thoughts that fixes our meaning potentials in that mode at that particular moment. When we return to that scrap of paper at a later time, our meanings may have changed and we find ourselves reconsidering what we have written. However, the material fixing of meaning has been *punctuated* from our ongoing thought processes at that moment and has been made available through a particular mode (writing) for us to consider at a later time.

The same process is at work when author-illustrators create picturebooks. Author-illustrators fix their intended meanings through selected modes of representation. The choices these artists make among various modes, in this case illustrations, design elements, or written language, are based on the *aptness* of that particular mode. Author-illustrators can better represent certain actions and concepts in illustrations than in written language and vice versa. However, all meanings must be fixed in a particular mode and material if they are to be realized and considered by others and communicated to the world. The designer is charged with selecting the most apt forms and materials from which to fix the intended meaning potentials.

The two primary representational systems mentioned above, written language and visual image, are governed by distinct logics; written language is governed by the logic of time or temporal sequence, whereas visual image is governed by the logic of spatiality and composition (Kress, 2003). The temporal sequence of written language, or the order in which words appear in a sentence, is important for understanding written text. For example, "The boy chased Lindsey" is very different from "Lindsey chased the boy." In visual images, the size, framing, placement, and composition of the contents of an image affect the meanings available. It is the spatial configuration of visual images and the temporal sequence of written language in multimodal ensembles that provide its meaning potentials.

The choices about what to represent in written text or in visual images are based on the concepts of materiality, aptness, and modal fixing. Illustrators use different materials and modes to communicate their ideas than authors. What can be done with photography, for example, is very different from what can be done through writing. In my own picturebooks, I chose to represent the natural environment of ponds, rainforests, and deserts through photography and written language. Describing the eating habits of a sea star through written language was easier than photographing it. However, it was easier to show what a sea star looked like with a photograph than creating an extensive written description. In addition, my publisher selected particular fonts and design elements to add to the overall presentation in my picturebooks, thus adding to the meaning potential afforded the readers of my picturebooks.

The modes available to designers change over time. Recent technologies offer designers new modes and materials for fixing meaning and disseminating messages. What may have been most apt at one point in time, like writing with organic pigments on papyrus, may be less apt at a later point like using a computer to write a dissertation. These changes have been going on for centuries and will only expand exponentially in the future, given recent advances in digital technologies. The media available to Gutenberg, Michelangelo, and Picasso are drastically different from those that are available to the average layperson nowadays with a personal computer and digital printer.

Affordances and Limitations

Each mode used in a multimodal ensemble brings different possibilities or *functional specializations* to the ensemble, and represents ideas and meanings in different ways. These possibilities are considered *affordances* of a mode, or their potential for expressing and representing particular aspects of our world and experiences. A poem is made from different materials than a marble sculpture, and what writers can represent through a poem is very different from what artists can represent through sculpture, photography, or painting.

The affordances and limitations of a mode involve social practices as well as material aspects and physical constraints. As we move from print-based texts to digitally based, electronic media, our ability to communicate across wider audiences becomes readily apparent. Producing and distributing novels, once exclusively the domain of large publishing houses, can now be done by a single author from the comfort of their home using a computer and an Internet connection.

Modes, although bound by conventions established through social practices, are also transformed through these practices all the time. No single mode provides an exact fit, readily able to represent all the meaning potentials a person intends.

Rather, modes like photography are altered in the new digital environments in response to the needs and interests of the designer, and the particular social practices in which they are used.

As software programs capable of integrating video, sound effects, visual images, design elements, and written language replace word processing programs, the social practices associated with these technological advances evolve as well. A shift from a Web 1.0 environment to a Web 2.0 environment signals changes in the roles of producers, publishers, authors, and graphic designers (Lankshear & Knobel, 2006). The once unidirectional sequence from publisher as producer to mass audience as consumer is radically altered in these new digital and global environments. These changes are as much due to technological and material advances as they are changes in the social practices and cultural contexts associated with them.

Design

Design is an active process of integrating and composing various modes for representing meaning potentials in multimodal ensembles. Design involves arranging various representational systems to fix meanings in the most apt forms possible. In other words, design goes beyond the use of conventional, stable, and traditional modes and semiotic resources, and becomes the process of translating a person's intentions and interests into the semiotically shaped materials that are the most apt for their purposes (Kress, 2010).

Any design or meaning making activity involves three interrelated elements (Cope & Kazalantis, 2009):

1. *Available Designs*—the use of existing, conventionalized semiotic resources and modes in the design of multimodal ensembles.
2. *Designing*—using available designs in new ways to design multimodal ensembles.
3. *Redesigned*—the transformation of existing designs and the creation of new designs for the production of multimodal ensembles.

Design is a process of working with existing designs or conventions, and transforming them into new designs based on the rhetor's needs, interests, and sociocultural contexts. Drawing on available designs and creating new ones, designers of multimodal ensembles both adopt and transform existing materials for their own purposes. Design is not about the reproduction of ready-made resources and modes; rather, it is about the transformation of these modes for the designer's purposes. This transformation gives agency to the designer as they make and remake new designs for communicating meaning potentials in contemporary settings. Conventions are standardized uses of particular resources based on interests, values, past histories of use, and the communicational and representational potential developed in a particular culture (Kress, 2010). In the process of designing a multimodal ensemble, the stable conventions of a culture are reconfigured to serve the needs and interests of the designer.

What was once considered *writing* is now viewed as *assembling*, or designing and composing various modes and semiotic resources into apt configurations for representing particular meanings. As our society moves from page to screen, the sequential logic of written text gives way to the spatial logic of visual image and new designs are possible given new means of production. These changes in how texts are ordered and composed alter the way teachers and students interact with these texts. Whereas readers once followed predetermined, singular paths in written texts, readers now navigate an array of choices when moving through digitally based multimodal ensembles. Visual cues for navigating these texts, for example, color, borders, frames, fonts, and headings, help students select from and organize their reading experience. Students no longer follow a single path set forth by the author. Instead, they design their own paths based on the criteria of relevance they bring to the screen (Kress, 2010). In other words, the paths students follow are created based on their needs and interests as much as the actual design of the website.

What is important to understand about design is that students do not simply draw from an existing pool of stable, conventionalized designs but rather from available modes and resources based on their needs and interests. For example, in place of the traditional five-paragraph essay, students may select a PowerPoint to represent their research findings, illustrate their chemistry homework, or go online to post a video focusing on their interpretations of an assigned novel. The variability in available and transformed designs provides the student with greater agency as they select and transform available resources to fit their own purpose.

CONCLUDING REMARKS

The opening epigraph from Kress and van Leeuwen (1996) serves to remind us that all texts are inevitably multimodal, and the modes that students select to represent their understandings have both affordances and limitations in representing potential meanings. Traditional theories and associated instructional practices of literacy education focusing on written language delivered through print-based texts have become inadequate as the sole systems of representation in today's culture. As society moves from the page to the screen, from written language to multimodal ensembles, our instructional frameworks must change to meet the demands of these new and multiple literacies.

These changes in modes of representation cannot be understood in isolation from social and cultural forces because they are bound together. A shift from the dominance of written language and the printed book to the increasing significance of the visual image and multimodal ensemble delivered electronically is also a revolution in the social and cultural institutions in which these representations function.

In many classrooms in which I have been involved in research projects, the images and written text have been understood as separate entities trying to do the same work. I have heard teachers asking students whether they liked the pictures better than the text, whether they learned more from the words or from the images, or whether they would like to add words to a wordless picturebook. I feel these questions are misguided because they pit visual images and written language in a contest of semiotic dominance that asks what mode works better. In much the same way, many people consider themselves visual learners, to which I have to respond, "not so much at the symphony!" We use maps to find where we are going, not because we are visual learners, but because maps are better suited to helping us navigate geographical landscapes than narrative stories.

It is important to remember that one mode is not inherently better than another; they simply do different things in different ways. What is important is understanding how different modes and semiotic resources are used to convey different meaning potentials and learning to use each mode to its fullest potential.

5

Elements of Art, Design, and Visual Composition

To imagine is to generate images; to see is to experience qualities.

—Elliot Eisner (1998)

In addition to the visual literacy concepts discussed thus far, students need to consider the basic elements of art, design, and visual grammar used to compose visual images and multimodal ensembles to better understand how these entities work. As educators, we need to help students experience the qualities of works of art and other visual images and use these experiences to better understand the features and meaning potentials of multimodal ensembles.

In their landmark book *Reading Images: The Grammar of Visual Design*, Kress and van Leeuwen (1996) proposed a *grammar of visual design* intended to "make explicit how the available resources of visual grammar form a potential for the production and communication of meaning through spatial configurations of visual elements" (p. 264). Like the rules of grammar for written language, a grammar of visual design is a set of rules or conventions for how the elements of a visual image or multimodal ensemble communicate and express meanings. Kress and van Leeuwen (1996) provide an inventory of elements and structures for producing and interpreting visual images. This inventory of visual elements and structures, along with Dondis' (1973) basic elements of visual communication, serves as a foundation for the concepts presented in this chapter.

The various elements of visual composition have a cultural bias, meaning that they seem to offer meaning potentials only when associated with a specific socio-cultural context, in this instance contemporary Western culture. In other words, a red rose may not symbolize the same thing from one social context to another. The structures described here are intended to offer perspectives for considering *meaning potentials*, not universal, stable meanings for individual visual elements. A border surrounding an image in one context may suggest something quite different from a border used in another context. The meaning potentials associated with each of these basic structures and elements should be seen as starting places for interpreting visual images and multimodal ensembles, not as universal, stable meanings realized in every context.

In this chapter, I will present a brief description of the basic elements of visual composition for teachers to consider themselves and subsequently draw upon to call students' attention to the various aspects of art, multimodal design, and visual grammar (see Figure 5.1). This list of basic elements is intended to serve as an inventory of the concepts students should be taught to attend to when approaching, navigating, and analyzing visual images and multimodal ensembles. This list is by no means exhaustive of the elements that may be considered; rather, it is simply a starting point to encourage students to see with new eyes.

ELEMENTS OF VISUAL ART

According to Dondis (1973), the basic elements of visual communication are the dot, line, shape, direction, tone, color, texture, dimension, scale, and movement. He suggested that these elements comprise the raw material of all visual communication and are used as a means for understanding complete categories of visual media or individual works, and for exploring their potential and realized success as visual phenomena.

Dot, Line, and Shape

The basic elements that make up visual art are the dot, line, and shape. These basic elements affect how visual images work and how students respond to them. Dots, lines, and shapes are all given different emphases by the amount of weight used to create them (bold or thin), their relative size (large or small), and their position in an image (top, bottom, center).

The dot is the smallest basic element of visual art. The dot is a position in space that can vary in size, placement, color, and number. Dots connect with one another and can lead the eye in certain directions; the closer the individual dots are to one another, the stronger the connection. Dots can be used in large numbers for shading effects, as in comic books, or as single entities drawing our eyes to certain positions on a canvas.

The line is the shortest distance between two dots. Lines are never static; they have a particular direction (horizontal, vertical, or diagonal) and always seem to be going somewhere (Dondis, 1973). Lines have come to mean different things based on their direction, weight, color, and length. For example, vertical lines suggest stability and are often used to separate elements in an image like the walls in a building, whereas horizontal lines are associated with calmness and tranquility and are used to bring various elements together like a bridge. Diagonal lines are more dynamic, leading the viewer's eye across an image, suggesting movement and energy.

Figure 5.1. Basic Elements of Visual Composition

Elements of Visual Art

1. Dot, Line, and Shape
2. Color
3. Size and Scale
4. Position

Elements of Multimodal Ensembles

1. Orientation
2. Typography
3. Borders
4. Motifs and Symbols

Elements of Visual Grammar

1. Representational Dimensions
a. Narrative Structures
b. Conceptual Structures
2. Interpersonal Dimensions
a. Contact—Gaze
b. Interpersonal Distance
c. Point of View
3. Compositional Dimensions
a. Information Value
b. Framing
c. Modality
d. Salience

Shapes are spaces that are designated by straight, angular, or rounded lines. Shapes can be open or closed, angular or round, and repeated in various patterns throughout visual images. Closed shapes create the illusion of a fence that keeps some elements in and other elements out. Traditional shapes offer particular meaning potentials in visual images. The three basic shapes—circle, square, and triangle—are often associated with the following meaning potentials:

Circle: comfort, protection, and endlessness
Square: stability, honesty, and conformity
Triangle: dynamic action, tension, and conflict

When shapes, lines, or dots are repeated in regular intervals, they create patterns. Patterns can suggest a theme or meaning potential depending upon how they are repeated or how a repeated pattern might be broken.

Color

Colors have long held a close association with various meaning potentials. As members of a culture, we connect certain colors with specific emotions and feelings. For example red is often associated with fire or anger, whereas green has been associated with envy. The various ways society uses color as a means of expression and communication is based on how colors are manufactured, and how colors have been used historically, for example their role in religious ceremonies or as trademarks (van Leeuwen, 2011).

Colors are always encountered as the colors *of something*, and the nature of that something influences our interpretations of it (van Leeuwen, 2011). In multimodal ensembles, colors are used to differentiate or frame visual elements, draw our eye to specific visual elements, connect us to historical periods or cultural settings, and make images look more realistic. The following chart outlines some meaning potentials associated with primary and secondary colors:

Red: power, warmth, anger, energy, activity
Green: nature, cool, calming
Blue: restful, detached, serenity, melancholy, passivity
Yellow: happiness, caution, warmth
Orange: fall, changing of seasons, fire
Black: scary, dark moods, night, depressing

Students need to consider how colors work in an image, going beyond noticing colors or being attracted to specific colors to consider what they might signify. Helping students consider how specific colors are used in an image and how they may affect their interpretations is a good pedagogical starting point.

Size and Scale

The size and scale of a design element depends on its connections to other objects. In other words, there is no *large* without a related *small*. Actual measurements are less crucial for determining scale than how large an element appears to the eye. In general, things that are bigger get more attention than things that are smaller. When artists and designers place a relatively large object next to a smaller one, the larger one is usually noticed and considered first. When two objects are the same size, they are perceived as more closely related and equal in power. Larger objects have more power, and tend to overshadow smaller objects.

Students need to consider what initially catches their eye when they are confronted with a visual image. They need to consider which elements are the largest and most dominant, and which are secondary and smaller. Artists use size and scale to draw the eye to certain things and in certain directions, and students need to consider how the use of relative size might affect their interpretations.

Position

In addition to the size of a visual element, its relative position also has associated meaning potentials. Things that are in the center are usually given more attention than things positioned on the periphery. Objects that are positioned above other objects, for example, characters placed in the top half of an image, seem to have more power over things positioned below them. More will be discussed on relative position in the section on *information zones*.

ELEMENTS OF MULTIMODAL ENSEMBLES

In addition to the basic elements of visual art, multimodal ensembles are composed of specific organizational, spatial, typographical, and artistic elements. These elements add to the cohesiveness of multimodal ensembles, and help bring unity to the work as a whole. Some visual elements are readily recognizable as meaningful or symbolic because of conventions associated with them, while others are less obvious.

Orientation

Print-based books are created in horizontal, vertical, square, and other shapes or *orientations*. Horizontally oriented books, also known as landscape formats, are wider than they are tall, and vertically oriented books, also known as portrait formats, are taller than they are wide. In general, horizontally oriented books are considered more familiar, soothing, and comfortable because they align with our horizontal, binocular plane. Since our eyes are aligned horizontally, humans orient ourselves to the world horizontally as they look out on it. For this reason, horizontally oriented images seem more natural and lifelike. Vertically oriented books are more dynamic and energetic. Portraits are usually done in a vertical orientation because the human body is more vertically oriented.

Horizontally and vertically oriented books are the most common. Square books are generally used for younger readers because they are easier to hold and handle. The square shape is comfortable, stable, and solid. Some books invert their orientation to suggest a particular meaning or theme. For example, the picturebook *Tops and Bottoms* (Stevens, 1995) opens like a calendar since the bear character lives in the top half of the book and the rabbit lives in the bottom half.

Another example is *Meerkat Mail* (Gravett, 2007), which opens and reads like a calendar from top to bottom rather than from left to right. When a book opens in such an unusual way, it immediately calls the reader's attention to the possible reasons the publisher chose to use such a unique style or orientation.

Typography

The typography and design elements associated with written language have taken on new forms and new roles in contemporary picturebooks (Serafini & Clausen, 2012; van Leeuwen, 2006). Rather than acting as a naturalized conduit for the communication of a verbal narrative, typographical elements have become an integral part of the story itself, a resource for authors, illustrators, and publishers that adds to the potential meanings of a multimodal ensemble. Different typographical versions of the same text can suggest entirely different meanings. Considering not only *what* is written, but *how* it is presented is an important part of interpreting multimodal ensembles.

Written language must always be presented through a particular typography or script. In other words, a text's typography is the vehicle through which written language is materialized. The choices made about which font to use and how it is arranged can add to the unity or coherence of a multimodal ensemble. Students need to consider various typographical features when they approach and analyze multimodal ensembles. A list of typographical features for students to consider is presented in Figure 5.2.

Borders

Borders are a type of visual framing device used to set certain visual elements apart from others. Borders around an image in a picturebook or magazine can be used to suggest a *window on the world*, calling our attention to certain aspects of the story and setting them apart from its other aspects. In many instances, a line is used as a border around an image, setting it apart from the written text. Some borders are presented as straight, hard-edged lines, while fading the edges of an image into white space creates a softer, more subtle type of border. When an image in a picturebook runs to the edge of the page, it is known as a full bleed image. When there is no border other than the edge of the page the viewer is drawn more closely into the events depicted in the image.

In art museums, paintings have borders or frames that set off the visual art from the surrounding walls. Borders show us where the image begins and ends. A border may also serve as a frame for the landscape artist, depicting certain aspects of a scene and omitting others. In the same way, the edge of the viewfinder in a camera serves as a border helping the viewer attend to only the included elements

Figure 5.2. Some Typographical Characteristics

Weight—the weight of a font ranges from thin to bold. Bolder fonts are more noticeable and powerful, where thin fonts suggest passivity and submissiveness.

Color—colors can be used to connect various aspects of written text, set off particular words, or suggest an emotional response.

Size—bigger fonts, like those used in titles, call more attention and have more power than smaller fonts.

Slant—slanted texts can be used to suggest motion or energy, or like italics, can be use to set off particular words.

Framing—the design of a font can be used to wrap around or frame characters and objects.

Formality—some fonts are more formal than others, where some are more playful and childlike.

of the photograph. Frames can also be decorative, like many of the gilded wooden borders used to frame Renaissance paintings.

Negative space can be used as a type of border to isolate and call attention to particular elements an image. The negative space is the area that surrounds many images in picture books and other multimodal ensembles. Negative space can be white, or it can be created through other colors such as black. The contrast among the colors used sets off particular features and provides a frame around others. In addition, the negative space can create a context for the objects and characters depicted. Single-colored backgrounds create an abstract setting for the positioning of characters.

In many picture books, borders can go beyond decorative purposes to offer additional information in expository writing or a parallel story in a narrative. For example, Jan Brett, Trina Schart Hyman, and Graeme Base often use the borders of the illustrations that accompany their stories to provide additional, often humorous elements to the written narratives. In this way, the borders become an element in the narrative, offering additional information through images and symbols.

Motifs and Symbols

Artists use visual symbols and motifs to convey meanings beyond the literal or denotative level. A *motif* is a recurring symbol used as a visual component that refers to a theme or expresses a particular meaning potential. Symbols and motifs can appear within visual images or as elements of a book's design. There is no guaranteed connection between a symbol or motif and a particular meaning. The connections between symbol and meaning are constructed in the social contexts of their use, and conventionalized over time. There are some symbols that have become so highly conventionalized we often take their connections to certain meanings as a given, for example, offering a red rose as a sign of love, or the use of a cross to represent Christian values. Many contemporary picturebook artists like Anthony Browne draw on pop culture icons as symbolic elements in their illustrations. Browne often uses street lamps, red hats, and iconic characters like King Kong, Mona Lisa, and Santa Claus to symbolize various ideas in his picturebooks.

A symbol is not a symbol until someone interprets it as one. Too often, students are left searching for symbols in literature and works of art without being given any tools to recognize or interpret them. Many of the most prominent symbols in today's culture are invisible to certain students due to their lack of experience or prior knowledge. Swastikas, peace signs, and certain types of clothing require an understanding of historical events to interpret their meaning potentials. It is important to teach students how to consider what might serve as a symbol, understand what meanings these symbols have had in the past, and deduce what they might mean given the present contexts.

ELEMENTS OF VISUAL GRAMMAR

Kress and van Leeuwen (1996) identify the elements of visual grammar in order to determine *how* things are represented or depicted in an image, but not *what* is represented. Images, like written language, are not neutral representations of an objective world; rather, the experiences and intentions of the designer or artist and the social contexts of the image's production and reception motivate the representations and our interpretations of them. Creating any visual image or multimodal ensemble requires the designer or artist to make decisions not only about what to represent, but also how to represent it.

In Kress and van Leeuwen's *Reading Images: A Grammar of Visual Design*, the authors drew on Halliday's (1978) three metafunctions to organize the various visual elements or structures presented. As described previously, the three metafunctions are: (1) the representational—how meanings are expressed, (2) the interpersonal—how the viewer relates to an image, and (3) the compositional—how visual elements are organized spatially.

Representational Structures

Representational structures are used to convey meanings, construct narratives, and suggest conceptual relationships. There are two kinds of representational structures used in visual images and multimodal ensembles: (1) *narrative structures* and (2) *conceptual structures*. Narrative structures relate participants and objects in narrative terms, namely, what they are doing, what is happening, or what events are unfolding. Conceptual structures represent participants, objects, and concepts in terms of what they are, how they are classified, or what characteristics they exhibit (Kress & van Leeuwen, 1996).

Narrative. Images depict narrative elements, for example participants, objects, settings, or actions, and set up relationships between participants and the viewer of the image. Participants in an image may act and react to one another, to inanimate objects included in the image, and to the circumstances in the scene depicted. In other words, images often depict something happening to someone, one participant doing something to an object or another participant.

When considering an image with narrative elements, it is necessary to begin by asking oneself who is doing what to whom or what object. A participant may be physically interacting with another participant or object, simply looking at another participant or object, or looking directly at the viewer. Each of these interactions forms what Kress and van Leeuwen (1996) called a *vector*. Vectors are imaginary lines formed between participants, objects, and viewers. Vectors focus our attention and develop relationships among the various participants and objects in an image. When one participant stares at or points a finger at another participant, it constitutes a vector. Considering the vectors and actions in a narrative image can help us understand who is doing what to whom, who is present and absent, and who is exhibiting power over whom.

Conceptual. Conceptual structures do not depict narrative events nor contain vectors or actions. Rather, these structures are used to classify people or things, and represent the relationship among visual elements. Family tree diagrams, outlines, and menus are types of conceptual structures. They represent the relationship among participants, concepts, or objects in terms of spatial organization. Visual elements in conceptual structures are often presented as headings with subheadings and related levels or hierarchies.

Expository texts use conceptual structures to organize how information is presented. Tables of contents, indexes, charts, graphs, and maps are used as ways of representing concepts and establishing relationships among the elements. The way we approach conceptual structures is very different from the way we approach narrative structures, whether we encounter them in written language or visual images.

Interpersonal Structures

Interpersonal structures focus on the relationship between an image and the viewer. During the Renaissance, *linear perspective* was created and used by painters to make their images look more realistic, bringing depth to their paintings through the use of geometric principles. This changed the way people interacted with images. Linear perspective forced the viewer to consider the world from a single vantage point with the horizon depicted as a vanishing point. In addition, the perspective from which an image is portrayed, or its point of view, and the distance from the viewer to the objects and participants also affect one's interaction with an image.

Contact—Gaze. Whether participants in an image are looking directly at the viewer or away from her changes the way that viewer interacts with an image. The initial *contact* or *gaze* viewers assume changes the attitude they take toward what is being represented (Jewitt & Oyama, 2001).

When the participants in an image look at one another or an object, or look away from the viewer, it develops a relationship between viewer and image known as an *offer*. In this relationship, the viewer of the image is considered an outsider looking in on the actions being depicted or is being offered something to consider. From this perspective, viewers are positioned as observers or *voyeurs*, focusing on the actions, objects, and relationships among the participants in the visual image. This relationship is less interactive than when the participants look directly at the viewer.

When a participant in an image looks directly at the viewer rather than into the scene or at another participant or object, the relationship is known as a *demand*. By gazing directly at the viewer, the participant is demanding that viewers respond directly to their gaze. Viewers are drawn to the participants who are looking at them and must consider what they are requesting. This is a more intimate interaction, and is used frequently in advertising and promotional campaigns to appeal directly to the viewer. The famous poster of Uncle Sam in a red, white, and blue uniform recruiting soldiers by pointing directly at viewers and saying, "I Want You!" is a classic example of this type of relationship.

Interpersonal Distance. The apparent distance of a person or object from us affects the way we see them, and the relationship that we develop with the participant or object. More intimate relationships are developed by bringing the world in for a closer look; whereas depicting people at a distance makes the viewer feel less connected.

Portraits typically represent people from a fairly close perspective, usually from the neck up. In order to see someone that close in the real world, one would have to stand very near to him or her. This suggests a more intimate relationship than someone depicted from a great distance sitting on a bench across a park. Advertisements often bring the viewer closer to objects or people depicted in an image than they would feel comfortable with in real life. When looking at an image, one must consider how the objects and participants are depicted and how close they appear.

Point of View. Another important element of visual composition is the point of view established between the viewer and the objects and participants included in an image. An artist may depict a particular character or object straight on, or above or below the viewers' point of view. When viewers are positioned to look up at a character, or other characters in an image are positioned to do so, the character being looked at appears to possess more power. In contrast, when viewers look down on an object or character, or when a character does the same, they appear to have less standing or power.

In the award-winning picturebook *Jumanji*, Van Allsburg (1981) portrays the house the characters are in from a variety of points of view. In one picture, the room is portrayed from the floor level. In another, the perspective hovers far above the participants. These bird's eye and worm's eye views change how we see and interact with the scene and the participants.

Compositional Structures

How various elements relate to one another, how they are organized spatially, and their relative position are referred to collectively as *composition*. Photographers, graphic designers, and painters pay close attention to how visual elements relate to one another in an image. Some elements are positioned next to one another to form a closer association, enhancing the overall theme of an image, whereas others are positioned to enhance the image by providing contrasting elements. Understanding how elements are positioned and the potential meanings of these positions is important when viewing visual images and multimodal ensembles.

Information Zones. Information zones refer to the positions or placement of visual elements, for example, in the upper and lower sections, the left and right sides, or the center and periphery of an image. In general, things placed in a central position hold more importance than things on the periphery. Objects and participants placed in the upper half of an image are considered *ideal* while things in the lower half are considered *real*. By ideal, Kress and van Leeuwen are referring to things that are more spiritual than earthly, more ethereal than factual, and more idealized than practical. For example, more powerful deities in religious paintings are positioned above other deities or in the center of a triptych (Kress & van Leeuwen, 1996).

The placement of visual elements on the left and right halves of an image also suggests different meanings. In Western culture, where we read from left to right, we also tend to view images from left to right. This means that the left half suggests what is old and given, while the right half suggests what is new or possible. For example, in "before and after" images the before image is almost always placed on the left so we read the images from old to new.

Framing. Framing is created by the use of negative space or borders around an object or participant to draw readers' attention to what is in the frame, or how the frame separates certain entities. Attending to what is included within frames and how they emphasize and separate elements of an image is important. Frames call our attention to particular aspects of the world, and help us consider these aspects in a particular context.

For example, the edge of a printed photograph serves as a frame. The photographer has decided what to include and what to exclude from the image. We see only those portions of the world that the photographer has decided to include. It sets our point of view and frames how we see the world. Comics and graphic novels use borders to separate events that take place sequentially.

Modality. *Modality* is the degree to which we are to consider the realistic or fictional qualities of an image or multimodal ensemble. Images with a high modality are represented as more realistic or lifelike, for example color photography. Images with low modality are considered more unrealistic or fictional. Cartoons or abstract art exhibit less modality than traditional landscape or portrait photography. Although cartoons and photography may depict real objects or people in different ways, it is the degree to which the representation is considered lifelike that determines its modality. In general, the closer the association is between representation and reality, the higher the modality.

When students approach a fictional story, they are often confronted with images of talking animals or cartoonlike characters. This level of modality signals a different way of reading than does seeing photographs of real animals or people.

Salience. *Salience* is the degree to which an artist or illustrator is trying to catch the viewer's eye to communicate the importance of a particular object or participant in an image. Salience also creates a hierarchy of importance among the visual elements of an image by using position, color, or relative size to call our attention to certain things. Salience does not necessarily relate directly to meaning, but it does suggest what an artist wants the viewer to focus on. Salience is a compositional process of calling attention to certain features in an image; the process of interpreting what a particular visual element of an image means is a bit more complex.

Three techniques that artists and graphic designers employ to call attention to particular aspects of an image are: (1) the relative size of the participant or object, (2) the use of color and contrast, and (3) the use of foregrounding and focus. These elements may be used by artists and graphic designers to call readers' attention to particular aspects of an image they deem to be important. Whether a character or object is bigger than another character or object, and whether he is in the foreground of an image, depicted in bright colors, or in sharp focus can make that character or object stand out or recede into the background.

In her wonderfully informative book *Picture This!* (Bang, 2000), Bang offers a framework for considering how the structure of visual images affects our emotional and affective response to it. She demonstrates numerous things students should consider when viewing visual images through simple drawings. A short list of these considerations from her work is presented in Figure 5.3.

CONCLUDING REMARKS

The frameworks offered by Dondis (1973), Kress and van Leeuwen (1996), and Bang (2000) allow us to consider the visual grammars, elements of composition, and meaning potentials of the visual images and multimodal ensembles that we encounter in our daily lives. Each of these frameworks challenges us to reconsider the structures of the images and texts we read and interpret. These frameworks also provide students with an observational guide for approaching, navigating, and interpreting the multimodal ensembles they are asked to work with in school settings. As students encounter visual images and multimodal ensembles, they need to be encouraged to consider not only the content of an image, but also its composition and organizational features. How things are represented and composed is equally important as what is included.

Figure 5.3. Considering Visual Images

- The edge of an image is seen as the edge of the imaginary world of the image, framing how we see the world as if through a window.
- White backgrounds are seen as *safer* and more comforting than black backgrounds.
- We are more afraid of pointed, angular shapes than we are of rounded ones.
- Larger objects dominate smaller objects when presented simultaneously.
- Objects of the same size, color, or shape are associated with one another.
- Negative space, or white space, can be used to isolate or frame objects.

Part II

CURRICULAR FRAMEWORKS AND PEDAGOGICAL APPROACHES

6

Picturebooks and Picturebook Theories

Picturebooks are one of the few quiet places left where a child can go to be alone, and to travel worlds past, present, and future.

—Dilys Evans (2008)

Long before children can read words, they are exposed to the visual images and stories contained in picturebooks. In fact, most children's first encounter with written narrative comes in picturebook form. Young children delight in the images contained in a picturebook as someone reads the words to them and performs the stories they cannot yet read for themselves. Often, young children's experiences with picturebooks are their first exposure to the world of literature.

Each page and illustration in a picturebook can be returned to, reflected upon, and studied at a pace that is not dictated by technology (Salisbury, 2007). In modern times, when it seems that everything students do is prescribed by advancing technologies, the act of reading and viewing picturebooks provides a space where students can determine their own pace and stop to explore the visual images and design elements in these multimodal ensembles as they see fit.

Picturebooks tell stories in a visual language that is rich and multileveled. Understanding the visual and design elements, codes, and literary and artistic devices that have influenced the production and interpretation of picturebooks enhances students' ability to appreciate and comprehend the subtleties of these multimodal ensembles. As students become immersed in these forms of visual art, each experience with picturebooks enhances all the experiences that have come before and changes the expectations for their experiences in the future. The more students experience these texts, the more they learn to appreciate the systems of meanings used in their creation.

Because the systems of representation used in picturebooks offer a variety of visual and textual resources for constructing and expressing meanings, teachers need to familiarize themselves with various approaches for analyzing and understanding visual images and design elements, in addition to the strategies they utilize for comprehending written language. Sipe (1998a) suggests, "when it comes to the visual aspects of picture books, many teachers may feel they lack the artistic

and aesthetic training necessary to talk with children and to guide their understanding" (p. 66). If teachers are going to be able to help students make sense of
the visual images, design elements, and written language of a picturebook, they
need to first be able to analyze and investigate these multimodal ensembles in
greater detail by themselves.

In this chapter, I would like to extend the previous discussion concerning the
basics of visual composition by focusing on one particular multimodal ensemble,
namely the picturebook. Figure 6.1 details the various aspects of picturebooks I
will be addressing in this chapter.

DEFINING THE PICTUREBOOK

Picturebooks are one of the most commonly used types of text in elementary
classrooms. You might notice that I am using the compound word *picturebook*
instead of using the two words *picture* and *book* separately to refer to these types
of texts; I use the compound word to suggest the unity or cohesiveness of visual
images, design elements, and written language that is part of all true picturebooks.

True picturebooks need to be distinguished from *illustrated books*. In an illustrated book, the illustrations serve as an added or decorative feature rather than
as an inseparable component of the story being told. In general, illustrated books
can be read and understood without the accompanying illustrations, though readers might lose some of the aesthetic qualities of the text. For example, some of
Roald Dahl's books feature black and white line drawings by Quentin Blake. The
illustrations contained in these books certainly add to the story, but the story could
be read and understood without them. The original stories written and illustrated
by Beatrix Potter would also be considered illustrated books. The illustrations in
Potter's books certainly add to one's aesthetic experience, but these texts could be
read and understood without the accompanying illustrations.

Picturebooks like *Voices in the Park* (Browne, 2001), *The Three Pigs* (Wiesner,
2001) and *Where the Wild Things Are* (Sendak, 1963) are examples of true picturebooks, blending visual images and design elements with written language in a
cohesive structure that simultaneously unfolds in both visual and verbal narratives.

Figure 6.1. Aspects of Picturebooks

1. Defining the Picturebook
2. Elements of Picturebooks
3. Picturebook Codes
4. Text-Image Relationships
5. Art and the Picturebook
6. Postmodern Influences

So much of the story would be lost if one were to read *Where the Wild Things Are* without Sendak's illustrations that it would be almost a different story. To read *Jumanji* (Van Allsburg, 1981) without the accompanying images would render the story almost incomprehensible. It is the cohesive unity of visual images, written narrative, and design elements that makes up a true picturebook.

Throughout this book, when I refer to *picturebooks*, I will be referring to the characteristics Bader (1976) expressed in her oft quoted definition from *American Picturebooks from Noah's Ark to the Beasts Within*:

> A picturebook is text, illustrations, total design; an item of manufacture and a commercial product; a social, cultural, historical document; and, foremost, an experience for a child. As an art form it hinges on the interdependence of pictures and words, written text, on the simultaneous display of two facing pages, and on the drama of the turning of the page. On its own terms its possibilities are limitless. (p. 1)

Her definition calls our attention to the commercial aspects of picturebooks, the aesthetic qualities of children's experiences with picturebooks, the synergistic relationship among the various visual and textual elements, and the sociocultural influences on the production and interpretation of these multimodal texts.

Picturebooks should not be viewed as a particular *genre*; rather they are a form of *multimodal ensemble* that encompasses many genres and literary styles. From my perspective, picturebooks are a unique literary experience, where meaning is constructed during the simultaneous unfolding of written language, visual images, and overall design. The visual and verbal narratives inform one another during the reading experience, allowing readers to oscillate back and forth between the textual and visual elements during their transactions with picturebooks (Sipe, 1998b). Each visual, textual, and design element enhances the other, with no single element revealing the meaning potentials of the narrative by itself.

Nodelman (1988) asserted the visual images in a picturebook show what the words do not tell, and words tell what the visual images do not show. Eisner (2008) contends that picturebooks are a form of sequential art, much like comic books and graphic novels. Marantz and Marantz (1988) called picturebooks a form of visual art, conceived as a unit that integrates all the designated parts in a sequence. Schwarcz and Schwarcz (1990) contend textual and pictorial narratives accompany, alternate, and intertwine with one another in picturebooks. Kiefer (1995) summarizes the relationship among visual and textual elements by suggesting they are simply interdependent on one another in rendering the narrative. Each of these conceptualizations of the picturebook addresses the interplay among text, image, and design and suggests the importance of the ensemble as a cohesive experience.

Sipe (1998b) describes the visual images, written text, and design elements of picturebooks as having a synergistic relationship, asserting that the meaning of the whole book is greater than the sum of its constituent parts. It is through the interactive nature of the various textual and visual elements of a picturebook that meaning is communicated and constructed. Picturebooks give students the opportunity to engage in an unending process of meaning making, as every rereading brings new ways of looking at visual, textual, and design elements.

Nodelman (1988) referred to the relationship or interactivity among visual and textual elements as a form of *irony*, where the visual images do not work seamlessly together with the verbal narrative; rather they are in a state of tension with one enhancing and also contradicting the other in a variety of ways. Because words and pictures do different things in different ways, the tension between the two seems an important concept to consider.

Moebius (1986) suggests unlike famous works of art hanging in a gallery, the visual images in a picturebook cannot hang by themselves, and do not fare well when they are extracted from the context of the picturebook. All aspects of a picturebook are carefully chosen parts of a whole, with each element of design adding to the picturebooks' cohesive nature. In a picturebook, the written narrative propels the reader forward as the visual images serve to slow the reader down to linger with the details included on each page. Doonan (1993) describes the role of visual images or pictures in picturebooks as representing real and imaginary worlds, as forms of expression, and as histories embedded in style and form that reflect the values of a society.

The basic premise of these various definitions and explications of what a picturebook is and does, is that the different modes of representation, words (written language), and (pictures) visual images, do different things in different ways. In addition to words and pictures, the design features of picturebooks bring these visual and verbal elements together to create unified entity.

Too often, reviews of picturebooks only give cursory attention to the role of images and focus instead on the quality of the written narrative. Picturebooks are too often judged as works of literature, rather than as multimodal ensembles that contain visual art. Picturebooks depend upon the interplay of words, images, and design, and need to be interpreted and judged as cohesive unities, not by their individual systems of representation. To attend to the written text in isolation from the visual images and design features is shortsighted and prevents students from appreciating the wonders of the picturebook form.

ELEMENTS OF PICTUREBOOKS

Sipe (1998b) has created an extensive list of picturebook terminology that I have adapted and added to for organizing the wide array of terms used to describe and analyze contemporary picturebooks. This glossary of terms also provides support for teachers to develop a vocabulary or metalanguage to call students' attention to various elements of picturebooks (see Figure 6.2).

This list serves as a starting point for developing a vocabulary to support students' analysis and interpretations of picturebooks. Naming these elements will encourage students to notice and discuss them, and consider how these features work as part of the multimodal ensemble. When teachers label the constituent parts of picturebooks, students will take on this vocabulary and begin to use these terms to analyze and discuss the texts they experience.

PICTUREBOOK CODES

Moebius (1986) explicated a set of codes embedded in picturebooks, calling our attention to the design and communicative aspects of, "marking the deeper channels of a modern art-form" (p. 143). These codes begin with the *presented world*, how the world is depicted in a picturebook. This depiction depends upon "certain conventions of recognizability and continuity" (Moebius, 1986, p. 143). The literal sense of an image or picturebook illustration provides students with a starting point for their experience, offering them a way in to the illustrations and a foundation for further analysis and interpretation.

The five codes offered by Moebius (1986) are paraphrased in Figure 6.3. This set of picturebook codes serves to call our attention to various conventions used to interpret picturebook illustrations and narratives.

Understanding these various codes supports students' interpretations and analyses of picturebooks in general, and through closer attention to the visual images and written narrative, students can gain access to the meaning potentials used in the creation of visual art forms.

TEXT-IMAGE RELATIONSHIPS

Creating a continuum of the relationships between written text and visual images may help students categorize various relationships between text and image, and come to understand the roles played by each system of representation in a multimodal ensemble. On one end of the continuum, there are books that contain virtually little or no visual images, like classic novels, and at the other end would be books with relatively few words, like wordless picturebooks. Of course, texts at the extreme ends of the continuum are not realized in actual practice. For example, wordless picturebooks are not published completely void of words; even these picturebooks include a title, and many novels are published with cover art and the visual aspects of typography. However, the continuum is nevertheless helpful in distinguishing between texts that rely predominantly on words on one end and rely on visual images on the other end in their presentation.

The relationship between images and words may be viewed as a type of *interplay* between the visual and verbal aspects of a picturebook. Although a more

Figure 6.2. A Glossary of Picturebook Terminology

Bleed: When the illustration extends to the very edge of a page, with no white space or border, it is said to *bleed*. When the illustration extends to all four edges of the page, it is called a *full bleed*.

Borders: Illustrators often design a border for their illustrations in a picturebook. Sometimes elements included in the border are used to tell more of the story, or to tell a parallel story.

Cross-Hatching: Fine parallel lines, usually drawn in black, are crossed with another set of parallel lines, to produce the effect of shading. Cross-hatching also gives an illustration a feeling of energy or vibrancy.

Cut-Out: An illustration which has no frame, but which simply appears against the background.

Double-Page Spread: An illustrator may choose to spread the illustration over both pages of an opening. This is referred to as a *double-page spread*.

Dust Jacket: The thick paper wrapper around the outside of a picturebook.

Endpages (also called *endpapers*): The first pages one sees when opening a picturebook and the last pages one sees before closing it. Endpages are like stage curtains, framing the performance within.

Epitext: Term for anything associated with a picturebook found outside the book itself.

Frame: In a picturebook, the illustrations are frequently surrounded by an illustrated border or white space, giving the impression of a framed picture. Sometimes, part of the illustration may "break the frame," seemingly breaking out of and overlapping the straight edge of the illustration.

Front Matter: The front matter includes publishing and copyright information, as well as the Library of Congress classification and the ISBN number. Sometimes, there is a note about what artistic medium was used to create the illustrations.

Frontispiece: A decorative illustration or engraving that faces the title page at the beginning of a picturebook.

Gutter: When the book is opened, the middle groove where the pages are bound is called the gutter. If an illustration spreads over both pages, the illustrator must make sure that important parts of the illustration are not set in the gutter.

Half-Title Page: At the beginning of a picturebook, a page is often included with only the title of the book.

Jacket Flaps: The parts of the dust jacket which fold over the front and back covers. Frequently, the front jacket flap contains a summary of the book, and the back jacket flap contains information about the illustrator and the author.

Figure 6.2. A Glossary of Picturebook Terminology (continued)

Medium: (plural, *media*) Paints or other materials (tissue paper, real objects, etc.) the illustrator uses to produce visual images or illustrations.

Montage: In laying out a page of a picturebook, an illustrator may choose to include several illustrations on the same page. This is known as collage or montage.

Motif: A recurring element, pattern, or design included in the illustrations or text of a picturebook that has symbolic significance.

Openings: Picturebooks are planned as a series of facing pages called openings. In a picturebook, the pages are rarely numbered. Thus, there is a difficulty in referring to a particular illustration or page. The *first opening* is considered the two facing pages where the text of the book begins, and the openings are numbered sequentially after this initial opening.

Peritext: Term for anything in a book other than the written or visual narrative. This would include the dust jacket, front and back covers, endpages, title page, etc.

Point of View: Every illustration is planned from a certain point of view, placing viewers in a certain position in relation to the scene in the illustration. We can be placed to look down on a scene, below the scene, or on level with it.

Recto/Verso: The right-hand side of a page opening (recto), and the left-hand side of a page opening (verso).

Spine: The bound edge of a book, which is frequently reinforced with an extra strip of cloth or cardboard.

Stock: The type of paper used in a picturebook. We can speak of glossy or matte stock, or stock of various weights, colors, and thickness.

Stamping: Visual images or letters are sometimes pressed into the front or back cover of a picturebook by a heavy metal die. If the image is simply stamped without any color, it is called *blind stamping*; if it is pressed in gold or another color, it is called *foil stamping*.

Text Box: The written text of a picturebook may be printed below or above the illustrations, in a plain white space. The designer may also choose to print the text directly on the illustration. As well, the text may be printed in a bordered box placed outside the illustration.

Title Page: The title page usually includes the title of the book, the author, the illustrator, the name of the publisher, and the city in which the book was published.

Typography: Illustrators or designers choose the typeface or font which is used for the text, the title, and other printed text in the book.

detailed continuum has been offered by Nikolajeva and Scott (2006), for the purpose of this book I will discuss three types of interplay that would be worthwhile

Figure 6.3. Picturebook Codes

Codes of Position and Size

> *Where* characters and objects are placed in an image affects how we interpret them. The impact of particular visual elements can be strengthened or weakened by their placement. Elements placed in the center of an image are given more attention than those placed on the periphery.

Codes of Perspective

> The rules of *linear perspective* and the placement of the horizon and vanishing point influence our point of view when approaching a visual image. How we are positioned in relation to the setting or characters in an image changes how we interpret the scene and various actions or events.

Codes of the Frame

> *Framed* and *unframed* images work in different ways. We look through a frame into another world, and become more closely involved with full bleed or frameless illustrations. In addition, the picturebook has a temporal frame—its beginning and its end, as well as spatial frames used throughout the book.

Codes of Line

> The thinness and thickness of the lines used to render characters and objects influences our understandings of them. Diagonal lines are more dynamic than the stable representations of horizontal and vertical lines. Thicker lines are more pronounced, with thin lines suggesting frailty or submission.

Codes of Color

> Color can be used to draw one's eye to certain elements in a visual image, affect the mood or emotional impact of an image, and is often associated with particular meanings in various cultures.

Source: Moebius, *Introduction to picturebook codes*, (1986).

to point out to students, namely (1) symmetrical, (2) enhancing, and (3) contradictory (see Figure 6.4).

The most frequently encountered type of interplay in books for young readers is the symmetrical interplay. In books with a symmetrical interplay, the words and images offer parallel or symmetrical information. However, a truly symmetrical relationship is theoretically impossible because written language cannot represent the exact same things in exactly the same way as visual images. Most picturebooks would be considered as having an enhancing interplay, relying on the interplay

Figure 6.4. Interplay Between Written Language and Visual Images

Symmetrical—visual images parallel the information provided in the text, and the written text provides similar information to the images, often repeating information in different representational forms.

Enhancing—visual images enhance or amplify the written text, bringing new ideas to what is written, and the written text offers additional information to the visual images creating a more complex dynamic.

Contradictory—visual images provide information that is contradicted by the written text, and the written text offers things that counter what is presented in the visual images. This oppositional interplay challenges students to consider the ambiguity among the visual and verbal elements and mediate among what is being offered.

of written language, visual images, and design features to render their narratives. Working in concert, visual images and written text offer an enhanced narrative from what a single representational mode could offer individually. It is not simply the artistic style used in the illustrations, nor the narrative structure of the written text that is important; it is the interrelationships among the various elements in a picturebook that create the dynamic aspects of this multimodal ensemble.

ART AND THE PICTUREBOOK

How something is represented in an image is just as important in the interpretive process as *what* is represented. The literal or denotative aspects of an image are only one aspect of the image that students will need to understand to make sense of it. The connotative aspects are influenced by the artistic style of an image as well as students' reading and viewing experiences. Different versions of the same story rendered in different artistic styles and techniques can yield quite different interpretations.

Art comes into the picturebook in a variety of ways, influencing students' experiences with these texts. Many contemporary picturebooks contain highly sophisticated, visual allusions to famous artwork (Beckett, 2010). This poaching, revisiting, or recontextualizing of famous works of art is characteristic of the postmodern world we inhabit (Hutcheon, 2000). While some works of art are reproduced faithfully in picturebooks, others are used as inspiration for a particular art movement or style.

In addition, fine art is often transformed to fit the narrative of particular picturebooks. For example, Browne (2000) transforms famous works of art, replacing human characters with primates throughout *Willy's Pictures*. These transformations help readers make connections between the story and the original work of art (see Figure 6.5).

Figure 6.5. *Willy's Pictures*

Finally, picturebook images and illustrations may be stylized after a particular art movement or technique. In Percy's (1994) wonderful picturebook *Arthouse,* the illustrations are influenced by a variety of famous artists, rendering the rooms of a house according to the style of these artists' original works. Whether reproduced, transformed, or stylized, fine art plays an important role in the creation of contemporary picturebooks.

All picturebook illustrators are trained in particular artistic styles or influenced by the world of fine art. They bring various techniques and devices taken from various art movements into the illustrations they create for picturebooks. Artists draw on techniques and devices taken from realism, folk art, surrealism, modern art, pop art, and other movements in their own work. The artistic styles and movements drawn upon by picturebook illustrators have different goals, intentions, and ways of representing ideas and the world. Understanding even the basics of these art movements and styles can support the discussions teachers facilitate in their classrooms and the interpretations constructed by their students. Without much effort, teachers can look up in online resources such as Wikipedia the basic premises of various art movements, for example, folk art or surrealism, and use this information to expand students' interpretations.

POSTMODERN INFLUENCES ON THE PICTUREBOOK

In recent decades, postmodernism has played an influential role in architecture, literature, fashion, and culture in general. It has also played an influential role in the creation and design of contemporary picturebooks. Postmodern influences or *metafictive devices*, for example, multiple narratives—where more than one character or narrator offers their perspective or story; nonlinear structures—where the narrative does not follow a traditional beginning-middle-end sequence; self-referentiality—where the text refers to itself as a work of fiction; pastiche—where several genres or text types are juxtaposed and blended together; and parody—where traditional texts and stories are commented upon usually with humorous intent have become techniques drawn upon by picturebook authors, illustrators, and designers.

Metafictive devices are designed to interrupt readers' expectations and produce multiple meanings and readings of picturebooks (Mackey, 2003). In addition, McCallum (1996) suggests the common element of postmodern literature and associated metafictive devices is their power to distance readers from the text itself, disrupting students' traditional expectations and practices, and positioning them in more active interpretive roles. Metafictive devices call students' attention to the act of reading, and challenge them to engage in the process of reading at a metacognitive level.

In addition, there is a playfulness associated with experiencing postmodern picturebooks, as authors, illustrators, and designers break traditional expectations of what a picturebook is and how narratives may be presented. This sense of playfulness and the disruption of students' expectations challenges them to deal with the openness and ambiguity associated with these picturebooks, and focuses students' attention on the structures, visual images, and contemporary designs of these wonderfully unusual multimodal ensembles.

Sipe and Pantaleo (2008) have detailed how various metafictive devices and design elements are important components in postmodern picturebooks. Ten of these characteristics are listed in Figure 6.6.

Picturebooks influenced by postmodern culture present challenges for students accustomed to the *introduction-complicating actions-climax-resolution* structure associated with traditional narratives. As they approach stories offered from multiple perspectives, students are required to go beyond literal meanings and attend to the various codes and conventions presented earlier in this chapter. Postmodern picturebooks are fun to read and will challenge even adult readers to navigate the structures and meaning potentials of these picturebooks.

Figure 6.6. Characteristics of Postmodern Picturebooks

1. Overly obtrusive narrators who directly address readers and comment on their own narrations.
2. Polyphonic (multi-voiced) narratives or multiple narrators.
3. Two or more interconnected narrative strands differentiated by shifts in temporal and spatial relationships, and/or shifts in narrative point of view.
4. Postmodern framing devices (stories within stories, characters reading about their own fictional lives, and mutually contradictory situations).
5. Disruptions of traditional time and space relationships in the narrative.
6. Parodies of other texts, genres, and stories.
7. Unusual typographical and design layouts.
8. A mixing of genres, discourse styles, and modes of narration.
9. A pastiche of illustrative styles.
10. Description of the creative process, making readers conscious of the literary and artistic devices used in the story's creation.

CONCLUDING REMARKS

Starting with the multimodal ensemble most commonly encountered in many homes and school settings, the picturebook, teachers can build a foundation for understanding other multimodal ensembles that students will encounter in both print-based and digitally based environments. Using picturebooks as the bridge from the print-based texts students have come to know in school to the digitally based texts they encounter more and more frequently outside of school, allows teachers to help students move from what they know to what they have not yet experienced.

7

Exploring Multimodal Ensembles:
An Example

Mr. Piggott lived with his two sons, Simon and Patrick, in a nice house with a nice garden, and a nice car in the nice garage. Inside the house was his wife.

—from *Piggybook*, Browne (1986)

To make the various perspectives and theories presented here more approachable and practical, and to demonstrate how a multimodal text may be analyzed, I offer an exploration of the written text, visual images, design elements, and multimodal composition of the contemporary picturebook *Piggybook* by Anthony Browne (1986). This exploration will serve as an example of how to analyze a multimodal ensemble using the strategies and resources detailed throughout previous chapters. Browne's book provides numerous opportunities for analyzing visual images, textual structures, and design elements across perceptual, structural, and ideological perspectives (Serafini, 2010b). Each of these analytical perspectives will be considered separately; however, in practice the distinctions across these perspectives blur and blend together in any actual reading experience. This chapter has been adapted from an analysis contained in Serafini (2010b).

Piggybook is the story of a mother, father, and two sons that focuses on gender roles and expectations, and how members of this family behave and believe they should be treated. When the father and two boys disregard the mother and the work she does around their house, the mother abruptly leaves home without warning. Subsequently, the house falls into disarray due to neglect and lack of domestic skills on the part of the male members of the family. In the visual images provided by Browne, the men turn into pigs both literally and symbolically as they fail to maintain domestic routines. The mother's ultimate return demands a revision of family roles and dynamics and increased respect for household chores and the mother.

PIGGYBOOK FROM A PERCEPTUAL ANALYTICAL PERSPECTIVE

Since *Piggybook* is not paginated, the book will be described as a series of *openings*, meaning a two-page display in the story sequence. The focus of the perceptual analytical perspective is to identify and label various visual, design, and textual elements; create an inventory of what is depicted; and use this inventory for further analysis and interpretation. An inventory of visual, textual, design, and multi-modal elements is the first step in the interpretive process.

Approaching the front cover of *Piggybook*, one is struck by the unusual title of the book and the image of what seems to be a traditional family posing for a portrait (see Figure 7.1). The border surrounding the portrait is broken by the heads of the two boys sticking out the top of the image. The shape of the book is a vertical or portrait orientation, which connects to the portrait-style image displayed on the cover. The colors of the image are bright, especially the color of the red jackets the boys are wearing, making them stand out in the image. A woman, whom one might assume is the mother, is carrying two boys and an older male, whom one might assume is the father, on her back in piggyback fashion. The two boys and the man are smiling, while the woman is not. The border of the cover image is green and black, and the color of the book is a light pink.

The second opening of the book presents the two boys and their father calling for their breakfast from a rectangular wooden dining table (see Figure 7.2). The father is hidden behind a newspaper, while the boys' mouths are opened wide as they call to their mom for their breakfast. The circle of their open mouths is repeated in the round dishes and cups of the table, and in numerous images contained in the newspaper the father is holding. The father and the two boys are asking the mother to hurry up so they won't be late for their important job and school, respectively.

The third opening of the book presents four sepia-toned images, arranged in four symmetrical quadrants, of a faceless mother doing the dishes, vacuuming, making the beds, and leaving for work. The mother is presented in monochrome in comparison to the brightly colored clothes worn by her sons and husband on other pages of the book. Readers do not see her face as she goes about her work. Three of the images are set inside the house, with the fourth outside on a sidewalk. In the fourth image, a small pig face is presented as graffiti on the brick wall behind the mother. She is dressed in a coat, standing next to a flagpole, as she looks in her purse for something.

The next spread is the eighth opening of the book. On the left side or verso, readers are presented with a mantel and fireplace with a copy of the painting *Mr. and Mrs. Andrews* by Thomas Gainsborough above the fireplace surround. The female character is missing from the painting, with a white outline left in her absence. Pigs are depicted in the mosaic tiles in the fireplace surround, fireplace tools, baseboard, and a vase and photograph on the mantel. The right side, or recto, of the opening, reveals a hooflike hand in a suit jacket holding an unsigned, handwritten note against a pig-patterned wallpaper stating, "You are pigs" (see Figure 7.3).

In the eleventh opening, the sons and father have completed their metamorphosis into human figures with piglike heads. The wallpaper, furniture covers, cans of food, and newspaper all resemble or contain pig faces. The painting of the *Laughing Cavalier* by Frans Hals has been transformed into a pig-headed cavalier. The male characters are shown rooting around for scraps, crouched on all fours roaming the floor. The text explains that one evening, as they were scrounging for something to eat behind the chairs in the living room, the mother returned. In the verso of the opening, the mother's shadow is projected casting a blue shadow on the wall, framed by the doorway in which she stands.

This inventory of the objects contained in the picturebook *Piggybook* is used as the foundation for the analysis and interpretations to come. The classification of the paintings included in some of the images required research beyond the covers of the text, while the rest of the descriptions focused on literal presentations and depictions of the visual elements of the picturebook.

PIGGYBOOK FROM A STRUCTURAL ANALYTICAL PERSPECTIVE

Approaching the cover of *Piggybook* from a structural perspective, it may be more effective for teachers to address each metafunction individually—ideational, interpersonal, and compositional (Halliday, 1978). For example, addressing the ideational metafunction, one would consider the way that characters are represented and the interactions among them. On the cover, the mother is carrying the father and two boys. The arms of the father and two boys encircle one another, while the mother's arms support the father and boys by their legs.

From the perspective of the interpersonal metafunction, the characters are positioned in a middle range of social distance, not too close and not too far from the viewer. It is like a full body portrait, where the viewer is positioned at eye level. The characters are all looking directly at the viewer, in a frontal orientation, demanding that the viewer interact with them. The modality of the artwork is realistic, yet not as realistic as a photograph.

Considering the compositional metafunction, a green and black border frames the characters included in the portrait. However, the boys' heads are breaking the border, suggesting a more intimate connection between characters and the viewer. The characters are positioned in the center of the image, increasing their importance or salience. They are also moving from left to right, suggesting a move from where they have traditionally been to where they are heading in the future.

Looking at the second opening, the boys are positioned on the left and right sides of the image, with the father positioned in the center attracting more attention even though he is hidden behind the newspaper. The boys' faces are looking up and off page suggesting they are talking to the mother in another part of the house. The viewer is brought in closer to the participants in this image. White space frames the entire image with no background provided.

In the third opening, the mother's face is drawn from the side and from behind. We are not given access to her face, suggesting she is less important, or an anonymous member of the family. The sepia-toned images suggest a traditional orientation, a connection to an earlier part of the 20th century when women had less social standing. The mother is clothed in monotone and depicted from a greater distance than the father and boys in the previous image.

The female character in the painting by Thomas Gainsborough entitled *Mr. and Mrs. Andrews* on the verso (left side) of the eighth opening is missing. The male character, Mr. Andrews, is presented with a pig head, and is staring wide-eyed at the viewer suggesting he is surprised by his wife's disappearance. The wallpaper and fireplace surround contain images of pigs and pig faces suggesting a metamorphosis is taking place. On the recto (right side) a pig hoof in a suit coat holding a note that reads, "You are pigs" is depicted. The pig faces that adorn the wallpaper are staring at the viewer with a circle shape to the mouth suggesting surprise or alarm.

Figure 7.1. *Piggybook* **Cover**

In the eleventh opening, the male figures, having completed their metamorphosis into pigs, are positioned on the floor on all fours drawn from behind with their rears pointing at the viewer. The mother enters the room and is framed by the doorway in which she stands. The reader sees her shadow from behind as she enters the room. The viewer sees what she sees. The shadow she casts across the door is Madonna-like, suggesting her return to save her family. The pig faces on the wall and in the wallpaper have down-turned mouths, suggesting concern and disappointment.

Each of the interpretations drawn from a structural analysis moves from the literal naming of the perceptual perspective to a consideration of the meaning potentials considered by the reader-viewer. The visual images serve as representations containing socially recognized conventions and schema for the viewer to draw upon when interpreting the meaning of the images and design of the book (Albers, 2007). There is no single, direct connection between the visual images and their meaning potential. The reader-viewer generates meanings based on her or his previous experiences, culture, and knowledge of social and image conventions.

PIGGYBOOK FROM AN IDEOLOGICAL ANALYTICAL PERSPECTIVE

It should first be noted that *Piggybook* is a commercial product intended for use by children, parents, and teachers in school settings and the home for pleasure reading. Browne brings to his picturebook his experiences, perspectives, and intentions in his production of the book. The publisher, for example Knopf, selects particular manuscripts to produce, and distributes their products through various commercial channels. In addition to the book itself, the context of the production of the images and text, its distribution, and how and where it is read or received are important considerations. For example, knowing the book was published in 1986 provides a social context for its reception. Reading the book in school because it has been assigned would be different from reading it at the library because some students came across it on their own.

Approaching *Piggybook* from an ideological analytical perspective, the image on the front cover suggests that a feminist perspective might be useful as an analytical frame. Questions such as, "Why is the mother carrying a grown man and two boys?"; "Is the image some playful reference to the title?"; and "What relationships in the family are working here?" can all be useful for interrogating the status and perceptions of the family members.

In the second opening, the mother is not shown in the image. Is one to assume that she is too busy cooking to eat? The traditional roles of domestic housewife and working father need to be contested and brought forth for discussion.

Figure 7.2. Piggybook

Figure 7.3. Piggybook

The family is portrayed as a traditional "nuclear" family, yet this type of family dynamic makes up less and less of the total population of most countries. Why is this family dynamic being portrayed as "normal"?

The images in the newspaper are reminiscent of the iconic, expressivist painting by Edvard Munch known as *The Scream*. The characters' mouths also seem related to young birds' mouths opening wide to be fed by their mothers. From a traditional family dynamic, the male characters sit at the table waiting to be served by the female character. Why is this relationship being contested?

In the eighth opening, the male character in the painting by Thomas Gainsborough has a look of surprise on his piglike face. The hooflike hand portrayed on the recto suggests the men have turned to pigs. This is a visual metaphor or direct reference to them being "male chauvinist pigs." The fact that the mother has left home, abandoning her family and leaving them to fend for themselves, with the male characters soon slide into domestic disarray, speaks to the roles that they were required to fill by societal norms. The neatness of the house at this point due to the mother's work habits and domestic routines will soon be a thing of the past as the men try to take care of themselves. Why are men portrayed as "domestically challenged" when in reality many are fully capable of taking care of a house, cooking, and cleaning for themselves and their families? This stereotypical portrayal of gender roles and norms should be interrogated and connected to the lives of the reader.

In one of the most revealing scenes in the book, the eleventh opening shows the mother returning to find her husband and children rooting around on the floor looking for scraps to eat. She is portrayed as a blue, Madonna-like shadow, framed by the doorway in which she stands. The father and two boys are positioned below her, squatting on all fours looking for food. The house is completely in shambles, representing the male characters' transformation from human to animal, in both of their physical features as well as their actions and speech. Is there a connection between the outline of the mother and numerous Renaissance images of the Virgin Mary? What connections can be generated from this similarity? Has she returned to save her family? Or has she been lurking outside the home to simply watch her husband and sons learn to appreciate what she does for them?

The roles traditionally associated with men and women are brought to light in this book. However, they are neither contested nor completely explained. The men find it useful to help out with various domestic chores, but only because they are forced into doing so by the mother's abandonment. The images of the mother change power positions with the father, at times being placed below, and then above him in various openings. At the end of the story, the wife goes out and fixes the car, a traditionally male role. From an ideological perspective, gender expectations, norms, and family roles needs to be an important aspect of any discussions of this picturebook.

CONCLUDING REMARKS

The analysis provided here is designed to help teachers and students understand how my perceptual, structural, and ideological analytical perspectives can be applied to a particular multimodal ensemble. My intention is to show the types of interpretations that are possible when teachers and students adopt a variety of perspectives. Helping students consider an array of perspectives enhances their comprehension abilities and allows them to analyze texts, images, and design elements in more sophisticated and nuanced ways.

8

Curricular and Pedagogical Frameworks

> Learning increasingly involves students in working across different sites of expression, negotiating and creating new flexible spaces for planning, thinking, hypothesizing, testing, designing, and realizing ideas.
>
> —Carey Jewitt (2006)

In this chapter, I begin by providing a curricular framework for organizing the way teachers support students' experiences with particular multimodal ensembles. Organized into three phases, namely: (1) exposure, (2) exploration, and (3) engagement, the curricular framework presented here gradually shifts the responsibility from teacher to student as students gain experience working with various multimodal ensembles and visual images. Each phase serves as a foundation for subsequent phases as students accept more responsibility for analyzing and producing particular texts.

The curricular framework suggests that teachers start by exposing students to a wide variety of texts and images to help them develop an understanding of a particular author, illustrator, artistic style, or multimodal ensemble, for example picturebooks or museum brochures. The second phase is an intensive exploration of the techniques and devices used to create various images and multimodal ensembles that help students shift from consumers of these texts to potential producers. The final phase of engagement invites students to produce a multimodal ensemble of their own for authentic and relevant purposes.

Based on the three phases of the proposed curricular framework, I offer an outline for a typical unit of study that will provide teachers with a pedagogical template from which to develop their own units. This template is provided for classroom teachers across various grade levels to develop units of study focusing on a variety of visual images and multimodal ensembles. This template will also be used as an organizational device for the units of study presented in Part III of this book.

A CURRICULAR FRAMEWORK

As noted previously, the curricular framework I propose includes three *phases*:

> *Exposure*—exposing students to a wide variety of visual images and/or a particular multimodal ensemble.
> *Exploration*—exploring the designs, features, and structures of various visual images and particular multimodal ensembles.
> *Engagement*— engaging in the production and/or interpretation of a particular visual image and/or multimodal ensembles.

Although the three phases of this curricular framework generally occur in the order presented, aspects of each phase build upon and blend in with the other phases. For example, even though the exposure phase focuses on reading and viewing a wide array of texts and images, students may be thinking about what type of multimodal ensemble they eventually want to create. In addition, as students begin creating a particular multimodal ensemble, they may realize that they have to go back and explore specific features in more depth to use them appropriately in their own creation. Each phase supports the other phases in a recursive manner; however, the lessons and learning experiences presented move sequentially across the three phases to support students development and expertise with a particular multimodal ensemble.

This curricular framework is designed to provide students with appropriate levels of support and challenge as they evolve from novices to experts, or from consumers to producers, working with particular multimodal ensembles. As teachers journey from the exposure phase, immersing students in a wide variety of texts, through the exploration phase, investigating these texts in greater detail, and eventually the engagement phase where students experiment with producing and disseminating these texts, teachers relinquish their responsibilities for interpreting and creating various multimodal ensembles as students accept more responsibility across these roles (Pearson & Gallagher, 1983).

The Exposure Phase

Before students engage with particular visual images or multimodal ensembles as potential producers, they must first experience them as consumers. In other words, students need to read a variety of multimodal ensembles from the viewpoint of a reader before they can read them from the perspective of a writer. During the exposure phase, teachers should invite students to read and experience the wide range of visual images and multimodal ensembles available to them in the classroom and outside of school to develop a sense of what is available.

Immersing students in a wide variety of texts and images aligned with a particular unit of study is crucial for developing a personal *map of the terrain* for the unit. This map of the terrain includes a working definition of the genre or text format being studied, a sense of the design features and textual structures employed, the types of visual and literary devices used, and the purposes that these texts serve in particular contexts. Students need to experience many examples of the visual images or multimodal ensembles under study to construct their personal maps of the terrain and develop a working definition of the characteristics of these texts. As students read and experience more and more examples in the first phase of a unit of study, they begin to get a sense of what these texts are and what they can do.

Although I've suggested arranging each unit around a *cornerstone text*—a prototypical example of the types of texts students will encounter within a particular unit of study, the variety of texts explored during this initial exposure phase helps students develop an understanding of the possibilities and practices involved with particular texts. For example, when students read and experience a variety of print-based advertisements, they begin to get a sense of what work is being done by these texts, how they are organized, and the different ways these texts are produced and consumed. During the exposure phase, students begin to understand the various audiences for these texts, how they are disseminated through various media, and the ways they are composed and organized. The exposure phase provides the foundation for the further exploration of the various textual, visual, and design elements and structures of multimodal ensembles that will occur in the next phase.

The Exploration Phase

In the exploration phase of a unit of study, students take a closer look at the elements and structures used to create and organize visual images or multimodal ensembles. In this phase, teachers should call students' attention to the variety of textual, visual, and design elements of the multimodal ensembles being studied. For example, in a unit of study on poetry, teachers might conduct lessons focusing on how senses are used to write poems, how metaphors and similes are used to compare things, how line breaks are used, how images are selected to accompany poems, or how anthologies are organized and designed. One of the key aspects of the exploration phase is the development of a specific vocabulary or metalanguage for discussing and analyzing the textual, visual, and design elements in particular multimodal ensembles. For example, students need to learn the names of the various parts of a picturebook, the visual components of an advertisement, the structures of a graphic novel, the relationships between written text and visual images in a brochure, or the visual elements used to create diagrams and maps. As students' understandings develop, so, too, will their language for discussing the elements and structures of the texts they are studying.

One of the primary goals of the exploration phase is for students to investigate and select a *mentor text* to use as a model or prototype for the multimodal ensembles that they will eventually produce themselves. Until teachers can actually hold a particular multimodal ensemble in their hands or view it on their screen, the models being used to demonstrate a particular genre or feature are too abstract to demonstrate to students. In other words, asking students to construct a traditional persuasive essay without offering a model text is too abstract. Teachers need to find actual examples of persuasive essays that exist in the world outside of schools. In this instance, the actual letters to an editor, magazine essays, newspaper columns, and speeches used in real-world contexts can be used as models, rather than some generic template for constructing school-based writing exercises. If teachers want students to create postmodern picturebooks or museum brochures, they need to provide examples of real postmodern picturebooks and museum brochures. The mentor texts selected become a model used to organize and produce students' specific multimodal ensembles.

By calling attention to the various elements and structures of a particular text or image, teachers help students begin to shift from the role of consumer to that of producer. Students learn about the techniques used to create the texts and images associated with the central focus of the unit of study, the affordances and limitations of the modes used in its creation, and the associated social practices surrounding these texts. With this knowledge in hand, students will be ready to create their own multimodal ensembles based on their knowledge and experiences developed in the first two phases.

The Engagement Phase

The engagement phase begins by inviting students to engage in the production and interpretation of their own multimodal ensembles or visual images. Drawing on the variety of texts and images that they have been exposed to, and the subsequent explorations of these texts, students are encouraged to use the elements and structures they have learned about to support the creation of their own visual images or multimodal ensembles.

In this phase, students are required to make choices concerning the design, production, and distribution of their visual images and multimodal texts. Students need to understand the affordances and limitations of the modes they select, and the choices available for representing and communicating their meanings and messages. The aptness of these choices is of particular importance as students make decisions concerning which modes will best represent their intended meanings.

During the engagement phase, students may need support from teachers in learning how to capture and process digital images, organize PowerPoint presentations, develop websites, illustrate picturebooks, or mix and revise video clips.

Teachers need to learn about various representational modes and digital media so they can better support students' engagement with them. Although students may bring a wealth of experience with some of these digital resources, teachers cannot solely rely on their own knowledge. It is a teacher's responsibility to understand how visual images and multimodal ensembles work in both print and digital environments as insiders before they can support their students to become insiders themselves. The engagement phase allows students to demonstrate and make visible what they have learned, and forces them to consider the audiences and purposes for their creations, not simply the medium used in its creation.

DEFINING UNITS OF STUDY

Units of study have been defined as: (1) a line of inquiry, (2) a curriculum map, (3) a teaching model, and (4) a way of connecting and exploring texts (Nia, 1999; Ray, 1999). I suggest a unit of study is a block of time spent reading, viewing, exploring, and engaging with a particular set of visual images or multimodal ensembles that includes a variety of learning experiences and curricular objectives that respond to students' needs and interests.

Units of study are organized around a central focus, and resources are subsequently selected based on their alignment to the chosen theme, topic, or genre. These units of study are designed to provide access to visual images and multimodal ensembles, allow students to immerse themselves in these texts, explore the elements and structures used in their creation, and engage in the production and distribution of similar ensembles and images. When teachers connect the instructional experiences and resources they provide to the experiences and interests of their students, they begin to develop a more responsive curriculum, one that takes into account the students they work with in addition to the learning objectives derived from a mandated curriculum or standards document.

Figure 8.1 presents the basic components of a unit study. These components are used as headings to organize the ten units of study in Part III of this book.

Central Focus

Units of study in the language arts are usually organized around a particular genre, topic, author, illustrator, theme, or type of text. For example, I have developed units of study focusing on mysteries, the Holocaust, the picturebooks of David Wiesner, fairy tales, transportation, and ABC books. The central focus of a unit of study may evolve from district curriculum guides, standards documents, or the interests of teachers and students. Reading and discussing specific images and texts aligned with a central focus better positions students to make curricular

Figure 8.1. Basic Components of a Unit of Study

Central Focus
Cornerstone Text or Visual Image
Learning Objectives
Launching the Unit
Lessons and Learning Experiences
Culminating Projects
Text Sets
Analysis Guides
Further Resources

connections across individual lessons and experiences. Making these connections across texts deepens students' understanding of the unit of study and provides a more cohesive and coherent approach to generating curriculum.

Cornerstone Text or Visual Image

A *cornerstone text* or cornerstone visual image is a text or image that is used as the foundation of a particular unit of study. Spending time exploring one text or image in greater depth provides the foundation that allows students to approach subsequent texts with deeper understanding. Each subsequent text in the unit may be compared with the cornerstone text, thereby allowing students to develop curricular connections and deeper insights throughout the unit of study.

For example, when studying the genre of personal narratives, I might spend four or five class periods reading, discussing and analyzing one selected picturebook like *Owl Moon* (Yolen, 1987) or *The Relatives Came* (Rylant, 1985) before proceeding to other examples of personal narratives in picturebook form. I could also select a particular visual image, for example the *Migrant Mother* portrait photographed by Dorothea Lange, to explore how images of the Great Depression affect our understandings of historical events. The time spent exploring one prototypical example in greater depth provides a scaffold for experiencing and analyzing other texts or images and eventually producing them. Rather than giving equal weight to each text or image across a unit of study, focusing greater attention on one cornerstone example demonstrates how to navigate and analyze all the subsequent texts or images in more depth.

Learning Objectives

In any unit of study, it is possible to address a wide array of learning objectives. For example, in creating a unit of study on contemporary picturebooks, I might draw upon various common core standards, my own understandings of picturebooks, and specific requirements found in my district-level curriculum guides to address the following learning objectives for this unit of study:

- Understanding how written language, design elements, and visual images contribute to meaning potentials of a picturebook.
- Constructing themes and connecting ideas across an array of complex picturebooks.
- Learning to attend to all the elements of a picturebook, especially design elements and peritextual features.
- Exploring the value in revisiting a single, complex picturebook from different perspectives.
- Applying reading comprehension strategies to understand and analyze picturebooks.

Indeed, there are many other learning objectives that could be included in this unit of study, based on a teacher's knowledge of the particular texts under study, the resources available, and their students' prior experiences. Common core standards and district curriculum frameworks can be used to help outline a unit of study, but the learning experiences teachers provide should remain responsive to the needs, experiences, and interests of the students. For each unit of study presented in this book, I will offer five learning objectives.

Launching the Unit

Each unit of study begins with introducing students to the texts, lessons, and resources that will comprise the unit. Getting students interested in the topics under consideration and helping them see the relevance and connections to their lives is crucial to a unit's success. Suggestions will be provided to help teachers introduce each unit of study and get students engaged in the experiences to come.

Lessons and Learning Experiences

In any unit of study, teachers need to decide what day-to-day lessons and learning experiences will be included and how these experiences will build upon one another to address the units' objectives. Individual lessons or learning experiences involve teacher-led demonstrations, classroom discussions, guided practice, and opportunities to reflect (Serafini, 2004). Some lessons and learning experiences will be specific to particular units of study, for example, understanding how endpapers relate to the meaning potentials of a picturebook; while others will support visual literacy skills in general, for example, understanding the effects of color in an image or the ways artists make certain things stand out. Five lessons or learning experiences will be provided for each unit of study in Part III.

Culminating Projects

Many units of study conclude with the creation of a visual image or multi-modal ensemble to allow students to engage with these texts and images as knowledgeable insiders and demonstrate what they have learned throughout a particular unit of study. Not all units of study require a culminating project, but being able to produce texts and images is an important component of the literacy curriculum.

Some examples of culminating experiences include having students create a personal narrative in print or digital form for a class book, having students make advertisements to get other students to stop bullying people, creating picturebooks on science topics to read to their kindergarten reading buddies, or designing a graphic novel for the classroom library. These authentic experiences allow students to work with the skills they have developed during the unit of study, and provide a framework within which students have choices about what they are interested in creating.

Text Sets

Developing quality units of study requires building an extensive set of resources over time as teachers encounter more and more possible texts and experiences to draw upon. In addition, combining digital and print-based resources of varying levels of complexity may require some exploration on the part of the teacher. Putting together a coherent set of resources or *text set* takes time. Working with other teachers and sharing resources is one way to gather the resources necessary for developing quality units of study. Some of these text sets are easier to construct, entailing, for example, gathering the picturebooks of a particular author or artist, while finding text sets focused on themes like escaping reality may require more exploration. Finding resources that provide students with varying degrees of support and complexity is a challenge. However, it is crucial to find as wide an array of texts and images as possible to help students understand the meaning potentials and literacy practices associated with the texts and images in a particular unit of study.

Analysis Guides

To further help teachers call students' attention to the elements and structures of the various multimodal ensembles, I have included analysis guides for each unit of study presented in the next section of this book. These guides are designed to focus students' attention on particular elements and structures they may not initially notice and to help them consider the potential meanings these elements offer. They are not designed as handouts for students to complete by themselves. Rather, these guides should be used selectively to widen students' perspectives and interpretive abilities, and for supporting students' abilities to approach, navigate, and interpret the texts and images included in each unit of study.

Further Resources

To help support teachers, I have included additional resources that will be useful as teachers are putting together their own units of study. These resources range from books that address the unit's focus to practical resources for implementing lessons and learning experiences. There is never enough room in a book to share everything you want to say about teaching, and these resources help point the way for teachers to go deeper into specific multimodal ensembles and theories of visual literacy.

AN INSTRUCTIONAL TEMPLATE

To better organize the units of study I have used in my classroom and the ones presented in the next section of this book, I have devised a template that includes the elements described in this chapter and provides a quick overview of each unit (see Figure 8.2). I have also created a year-long planning template that may be used to get a sense of how various units of study may be organized throughout a school year (see Figure 8.3).

CONCLUDING REMARKS

Given the ubiquitous nature of visual images and multimodal ensembles, one might think that teachers are already prepared to help students navigate and interpret the complex and sophisticated nature of visual images and multimodal ensembles. However, many teachers are not yet comfortable with the challenges that digitally based and multimodal texts present for students. Most of the current population of teachers are not *digital natives* like so many of their students and may not be as comfortable with the digital environments that students engage with outside schools (Brumberger, 2011). As teachers begin to develop a curriculum and pedagogical framework to support the navigation, interpretation, and analysis of visual images and multimodal ensembles, they need to expand their

Figure 8.2. Unit of Study Template

Central Focus
Cornerstone Text or Visual Image
Learning Objectives
Launching the Unit
Lessons and Learning Experiences
Culminating Projects

Figure 8.3. Year-Long Planning Sheet

Central Focus	Possible Learning Objectives	Time Span	Culminating Experience

comfort level with various forms of technology in addition to exploring interesting instructional resources for developing their day-to-day lessons.

A shift from consumer to producer requires an extensive exploration of the various components, structures, and designs of particular visual images and multimodal ensembles. As students begin to learn the techniques necessary for their production, the affordances and limitations of various modes and the social practices associated with any given semiotic resource, they evolve from consumer to producer. This evolution requires making the shift from what a multimodal ensemble is, to how it is used, how it works, and what it can do for the producer.

L

Part III

UNITS OF STUDY

Exploring Postmodern Picturebooks

Central Focus of the Unit

Postmodern picturebooks draw upon a variety of metafictive devices, for example multiple narrators, nonlinear sequences, parody, and self-referentiality in their design. These unusual picturebooks challenge readers to break from their traditional patterns and expectations for reading picturebooks and address the unique features and structures of these multimodal texts.

Metafictive devices call students' attention to the act of reading, and challenge them to engage in the process of reading at a metacognitive level. Because these texts have unique designs and structures, students' reading processes are made apparent as they wrestle with unexpected twists and turns. In addition, there is a playfulness associated with experiencing postmodern picturebooks, as authors, illustrators, and designers break traditional expectations for what a picturebook is and how narratives may be presented. This sense of playfulness and the disruption of students' expectations challenge them to deal with the openness and ambiguity associated with these picturebooks, and focuses students' attention on the structures, visual images, and contemporary designs of these wonderfully unusual multimodal ensembles.

This unit will focus on the literary devices used to create postmodern picturebooks, and the shift in expectations and strategies necessary for interpreting these texts. As students encounter the unique structures and elements of postmodern picturebooks, they will need support to develop their understandings of how these books work and what strategies will be helpful in making sense of these unpredictable texts.

Cornerstone Text or Visual Image

Voices in the Park (Browne, 2001) is a story of four characters' journey to an English park told in four sections from the perspective of each of the four characters. Browne uses multiple narrators to offer different versions of a trip to a local park, creating tension among each character's perspective on the events. A mother and her son, and a father and his daughter each have different views of the park and their outlook on life. Issues of race, class, and gender are developed as each story unfolds and is considered in light of the other versions of the events.

Learning Objectives

- Understand how various metafictive and literary devices are used in postmodern picturebooks.
- Learn to tolerate the ambiguity associated with a story told through multiple narrators.
- Use strategies to understand the differences among the perspectives presented in postmodern picturebooks.
- Understand the ironic or contradictory relationship between images and written narrative that is part of many postmodern picturebooks.
- Develop strategies for analyzing the peritextual elements of postmodern picturebooks, including the covers, title pages, endpapers, and other elements.

Launching the Unit

Spending a week with the cornerstone text *Voices in the Park* would be an effective way to launch this unit. Reading the book aloud and having a discussion about its plot and perspectives for a couple of days is a good way to begin. After the initial read-alouds and discussions, taking the book apart and presenting it in storyboard fashion on a wall of the classroom adds another dimension to the discussions. Make color copies of the book *Voices in the Park* (while for classroom use be aware that copyright infringement may be an issue when photocopying texts) and lay it out on a wall or across a table displaying each character's story in four parallel lines. This storyboard display allows students to see each character's visual story simultaneously and compare and contrast each character's perspectives with one another.

Next, I would have some students practice reading the four voices separately and present the book to the rest of the class in readers' theater format. Four students can be selected to perform the four voices in the book and given time to interpret each perspective before presenting their part to the class. Have students practice developing a tone of voice or way of speaking for each character that represents their interpretation of the character's way of life. For example, Charles seems to be rather timid and could be read in a milder voice, whereas the father seems down and out and could be read in a depressed tone. Students then get to listen to the book during readers' theater and discuss how the characters were portrayed and how this adds to their own interpretations. Students can consider whether they agree with the way the character was interpreted by the performer and how their interpretations might differ.

During the unit of study, a chart listing the various metafictive and literary devices used in postmodern picturebooks might be created. In addition, students could work together to construct a working definition of what constitutes a postmodern picturebook. As the unit progresses, a list of reading and viewing strategies for approaching and interpreting the picturebooks encountered would also be constructed with the students.

Lessons and Learning Experiences

1. *Surrealist Art Forms*—Using some examples of surrealist art, for example *The Treachery of Images* by Rene Magritte, or Salvador Dali's *The Persistence of Memory*, discuss with students the basic tenets of surrealism (easily found on Wikipedia or art history books) and how these tenets effected the way Browne and other picturebook artists presented their illustrations.
2. *Postmodern Devices*—Throughout the unit, students will be exposed to a variety of postmodern or metafictive devices. Mini-lessons discussing how each of the selected devices are used are important to include. Select particular postmodern picturebooks from the list provided to highlight each device.
3. *Visual Image Analysis*—Have students select a particular page from the book *Voices in the Park* and analyze the image using a double entry or T-chart with the headings: What Do You Notice? What Might It Mean? The goal in this lesson is to move students from simply noticing elements of the visual images to interpreting them as meaningful aspects of the narrative.
4. *Addressing Multiple Narratives*—The multiple narrative structure of *Voices in the Park* requires readers to consider multiple perspectives as they interpret each individual version of the story. As each perspective offers a different version of events, readers must be able to put themselves in different positions to consider different characters' points of view. The sense of ambiguity that is part of many of these postmodern picturebooks challenges readers to suspend closure of these narratives. Students must be willing to read them several times and consider the many possible meanings before reaching any conclusions.
5. *Motif and Symbol Analysis*—Browne draws on images and icons taken from pop culture and fine art to construct motifs and symbols in his illustrations. For example, in the cornerstone text, *Voices in the Park*, discuss with students what the symbol of the red hat might mean. Then, have students identify a particular icon or image and discuss why

Browne may have put it in his illustrations. Have students do some research on the connections among what is happening in the story and the use of these iconic images in the world.

Culminating Projects

Have students create their own postmodern picturebooks using some of the metafictive elements they have encountered throughout the unit. Students would select from the metafictive and literary devices used in the picturebooks across the unit to create a picturebook. Students would select a mentor text to use as a scaffold for their own writing.

Text Set

Ahlberg, J., & Ahlberg, A. (1986). *The jolly postman or other people's letters*. Boston: Little, Brown and Company.

Browne, A. (1991). *Willy's pictures*. Cambridge, MA: Candlewick.

Browne, A. (1983). *Gorilla*. London: Julia MacRae Books.

Browne, A. (1997). *The tunnel*. London: Walker Books.

Browne, A. (2001). *Voices in the park*. New York: DK Publishing.

Burningham, J. (1978). *Time to get out of the bath, Shirley*. London: Jonathan Cape.

Child, L. (2000). *Beware of the storybook wolves*. New York: Scholastic.

Child, L. (2002). *Who's afraid of the big bad book?* New York: Hyperion.

Gravett, E. (2006). *Wolves*. New York: Simon & Schuster.

Lendler, I. (2005). *An undone fairy tale*. New York: Simon & Schuster.

Macauley, D. (1990). *Black and white*. Boston, MA: Houghton Mifflin.

Macauley, D. (1995). *Shortcut*. Boston, MA: Houghton Mifflin.

McGuire, R. (1997). *What's wrong with this book?* New York: Viking.

Scieszka, J. (1992). *The stinky cheese man and other fairly stupid tales*. New York: Viking.

Wiesner, D. (2001). *The three pigs*. New York: Houghton Mifflin.

Analysis Guide—Postmodern Picturebooks

1. Approaching a Postmodern Picturebook:

- Pick up the picturebook, attending to the size, format (horizontal or vertical), materials used in construction of book (papers, graphics).
- Consider the author of the text and the artist. What media is used in the illustrations? What fonts are selected? Where is the text located on the page? Borders, etc.
- Look at the cover, title, and illustrations. What expectations are set up for you as you approach the picture book? What does the cover, title, and illustrations suggest?

- What is included in the peritext? The dedication, title page, author's note, summary statement, etc.

2. Read through the picturebook more deliberately, marking important aspects you want to consider. After your second reading, consider the following questions:

- What is the overall structure of the text?
- How does the opening of the story compare with the closing of the story?
- How do the illustrations relate to the text?
- Words propel the reader forward and images slow us down. How did this tension between reading and viewing affect your experience?
- What kind of gaps does the author/illustrator leave for the reader to fill in? Are details purposefully left out to create tension?
- How does the story flow from page to page? Are there borders that separate things or does it cross over in language and image from page to page?
- Is there a relationship between form and content? Does the design of the book add to the content being presented? How?
- What themes were constructed as you read?

3. Analyzing Visual Images and Design in Postmodern Picturebooks

- Begin by considering the format of the images and their placement in the picturebook. Where is the text located? Is it within the image or separated by borders or white space? Why?
- Are the illustrations double-page spreads, single page images, collages, overlapping images, or portraits?
- Consider the series of images in the picturebook. Do the images change over the course of the book? Do they get bigger, smaller, change?

4. Select a particular image to consider. Ask the following:

- What is foregrounded and in the background?
- Consider the "path" your eyes follow as you approach the image. What catches your eye first? Why is that element salient?
- What colors dominate the image? What effect does this have on you as reader?
- Consider the use of white (negative) space. Are the illustrations framed or full bleed? How does this position you as a viewer?
- What is the artist trying to get you to look at through leading lines, colors, contrast, gestures, lighting?
- Are there any recurring symbols or motifs in the images?
- How are the images framed? Are there thick borders or faded edges?

- Consider size and scale. What is large? Why are certain elements larger than others? Does this add to meanings of power, control?
- Consider the viewers's point of view. Do characters directly gaze or address the viewer? Are the characters close up or distanced? How does point of view add to relationships with the characters?

Further Resources

Anstey, M. (2002). More than cracking the code: Postmodern picture books and new literacies. In G. Bull & M. Anstey (Eds.), *Crossing the boundaries* (pp. 87–105). Frenchs Forest, NSW: Prentice Hall.

Goldstone, B. P. (2001). Whaz up with our books? Changing picture book codes and teaching implications. *The Reading Teacher, 55*(4), 362–370.

Goldstone, B. P. (2004). The postmodern picture book: A new subgenre. *Language Arts, 81*(3), 196–204.

Serafini, F. (2008). The pedagogical possibilities of postmodern picturebooks. *The Journal of Reading, Writing and Literacy, 2*(3), 23–41.

Serafini, F. (2009). Understanding visual images in picturebooks. In J. Evans (Ed.), *Talking beyond the page: Reading and responding to contemporary picturebooks* (pp. 10–25). London, UK: Routledge.

Sipe, L. R. (1998). How picture books work: A semiotically framed theory of text-picture relationships. *Children's Literature in Education, 29*(2), 97–108.

Sipe, L. R., & Pantaleo, S. (Eds.). (2008). *Postmodern picturebooks: Play, parody, and self-referentiality.* New York: Routledge.

Exploring Wordless Picturebooks

Central Focus of the Unit

Wordless picturebooks rely primarily on visual images in sequence to tell a story. This picturebook format does include some written language, for example a title, usually some book jacket blurbs, and some publisher's information. However, wordless picturebooks focus on visual images and design elements in sequence to present a visual narrative. The narratives in wordless picturebooks are considered more open-ended since no written text is available to anchor the meanings of the visual images. In these picturebooks, the artist places a priority on the visual images in sequence to tell a story that often includes a detailed setting, characters' emotions presented through facial expression and gestures, a sequence of events or plot, and design elements that add to the cohesive nature of the ensemble.

The lack of interplay between image and text may challenge young readers as they read back and forth through the picturebook to consider its meaning potentials. The composition of the visual narrative is more ambiguous and provides a less restricted reading path through the text. In other words, though the images are presented in a particular order, readers are free to consider and reconsider them in other sequences. There is a sense of playfulness that is often associated with the open structures of wordless picturebooks. Students are invited to serve as coauthor as they construct a story from the sequence of images.

Cornerstone Text or Visual Image

Flotsam (Wiesner, 2006) is a Caldecott Award–winning wordless picturebook that tells the story of a boy's adventures at the beach. The boy spends his day exploring the creatures and objects along the beach until a camera washes ashore. He develops the film that is inside the camera and learns of other worlds and adventures as he looks through the photographs. The story takes the boy into other worlds, both real and imaginary, and circles back to his own life along the shore.

Learning Objectives

- Understand how narrative sequences are portrayed in wordless picturebooks.

- Determine the possible reading paths in wordless picturebooks.
- Consider any recurring patterns and visual symbols used in wordless picturebooks, especially the symbols and images used in the peritextual elements, including the cover, title page, dust jacket, and endpapers.
- Understand how gutters and panels are used to present a narrative sequence of images and how these design elements affect the narrative.
- Understand what happens in the gutters between the illustrated panels in wordless picturebooks.

Launching the Unit

Reading *Flotsam* and talking about the story is an excellent way to begin this unit of study. As you "read aloud" the book to students consider how you present the sequence of images. Since there are no words to read aloud, additional time must be provided for students to explore the images in greater detail. Reading the title and any information provided on the book jacket or author-illustrator note can help students prepare for the visual narrative within. Discussing the meaning of the word *flotsam* and how this word relates to the story is also a good place to start.

The peritextual elements of *Flotsam* are important to consider before reading and sharing the book with students. The trade, hardcover version of the book comes with a dust jacket. When you remove the jacket, you will notice an embossed octopus on the front cover. In addition, consider how the color and texture of the endpapers suggests the setting of a beach and the ocean. A close look at the eye of the fish on the front cover reveals a reflection of a camera that becomes an important element and motif used throughout the story. The title page illustrations also deserve some exploration before beginning to read the book itself.

Working with *Flotsam*, I suggest spending a few days considering how the panels and gutters are used to present the narrative sequence and what reading paths are offered through the book's design. Once the panels have been discussed, I recommend considering one or two visual images in greater detail. The opening image, a close-up image of an eye looking at a hermit crab, suggests the reader will be directed to look closely at various images presented. The second opening presents a setting in which the boy is looking at the crab and what surrounds him. In the third opening, Wiesner begins to offer images contained in panels requiring readers to decide the order the images will be considered. As we progress further into the book, the borders change when the images become photographs that have been developed from the camera found by the boy. Talking with students about these design features helps support their interpretations.

It is important for readers to experience a variety of these texts before they are expected to explore the particular devices and visual elements that make up this genre. Some wordless picturebooks are very simple and tell a story in a linear sequence, for example, *Pancakes for Breakfast* (dePaola, 1978), *A Ball for*

Daisy (Raschka, 2011), *The Lion and the Mouse* (Pinkney, 2009), and *Wave* (Lee, 2008). The narratives in these picturebooks proceed from beginning to end in linear fashion, providing a good starting point for readers to experience wordless picturebooks. Other examples, such as *The Arrival* (Tan, 2007) and *Time Flies* (Rohmann, 1997) offer more complicated narrative sequences, and may require more time and experience to understand them.

Lessons and Learning Experiences

1. *Narrative Sequence*—One of the most important lessons in this unit would be to explore the concept of sequencing of images and how this occurs in wordless picturebooks. Reading across frames from left to right and then down is important when approaching these picturebooks. How many images are used on each opening and what order to approach them is also an important consideration. Take a single page and discuss the order of the images presented. How would the story change if the order of the images were changed or reversed?

2. *Gutters and Image Breaks*—What happens in between the sequentially ordered visual images in a wordless picturebook is just as important as what happens within particular images. The space between framed images or *panels* in a wordless picturebook is called the *gutter*. In the gutter between images time may pass, settings may change, flashbacks may occur, and new perspectives may be offered on the same event. In comics and graphic novels, the author-illustrator may use text boxes to signal what has changed from panel to panel. In wordless picturebooks, this is often left to the reader to infer. Locate several panels from a variety of wordless picturebooks that employ different uses for the gutter, for example time passing, setting changing, sequence interruption, or perspective changing. Discuss what is happening in these different gutters and explore strategies for understanding the clues to follow these transitions.

3. *Visual Point of View*—*Flotsam* (2006) is a good example of how an artist may change the point of view provided to the reader in the panels presented. In this book, Wiesner brings the viewer in close to and way above the events taking place. By varying the social distance between viewer and image, we move in and out of the story, considering the events from a variety of perspectives. Taking several images from *Flotsam* and other wordless picturebooks, have students consider how much of the scene is being presented and how this affects the readers' interpretations and understandings of the story. By considering an array of visual points of view, readers come to see that it is not just *what* is presented in each panel, but *how* it is presented that is important to consider.

4. *Framing Devices*—Each panel in a wordless picturebook is usually surrounded by a black line that serves as a frame for a particular panel. These lines may be thin or bold, and they work to separate the panels into a narrative sequence. Other framing devices, for example, the camera lens and magnifying glass in *Flotsam*, are used to separate and connect aspects of individual visual images. The photographs that were developed from the Melville Underwater Camera in the story have different frames or borders from the other visual images. How does this frame change the way we experience these images? Using *Flotsam* as an example, consider how the frames of other wordless picturebooks are used and how they add to the narrative.

5. *Structures of Wordless Picturebooks*—Different wordless picturebooks are presented and structured in different ways. Using *The Snowman* (Briggs, 1978) and *A Ball for Daisy* (Raschka, 2011) discuss how white space and panels are used in different ways to organize the visual narrative.

Culminating Projects

It would seem obvious that having students create a wordless picturebook would be an appropriate culminating experience, and I agree. However, the focus is on telling a story without textual features, and there are many more possibilities than simply creating a wordless picturebook. Possibly creating wordless brochures, animated short stories without sound, comic strips with no text, or captionless cartoons would be another option. The focus is on visual storytelling, and that can be accomplished in a number of ways. How do artists tell stories through sequential images? Hieroglyphs and cave paintings also tell stories through visual images and should be seen as other possible experiences worthy of exploring.

Text Sets

Anno, M. (1997). *Anno's journey*. New York: Puffin.
Bang, M. (1996). *The grey lady and the strawberry snatcher*. New York: Aladdin.
Banyai, I. (1995). *Zoom*. New York: Viking.
Banyai, I. (1995). *Re-Zoom*. New York: Viking.
Briggs, R. (1978). *The snowman*. New York: Random House.
dePaola, T. (1978). *Pancakes for breakfast*. New York: Harcourt.
Goffin, J. (1991). *Oh!* New York: Harry N. Abrams.
Lee, S. (2008). *Wave*. San Francisco: Chronicle Books.
Lehman, B. (2004). *The red book*. Boston: Houghton Mifflin.
Pinkney, J. (2009). *The lion and the mouse*. New York: Little Brown.
Raschka, C. (2011). *A ball for daisy*. New York: Schwartz and Wade.
Rohmann, E. (1997). *Time flies*. New York: Dragonfly Books.
Smith, L. (1988). *Flying jake*. New York: Aladdin.

Spier, P. (1977). *Noah's ark*. New York: Doubleday.
Tan, S. (2007). *The arrival*. New York: Arthur A. Levine.
Thomson, B. (2010). *Chalk*. Tarrytown, NY: Marshall Cavendish.
Wiesner, D. (1988). *Free fall*. New York: Mulberry Books.
Wiesner, D. (1991). *Tuesday*. New York: Clarion Books.
Wiesner, D. (1999). *Sector 7*. New York: Clarion Books.
Wiesner, D. (2006). *Flotsam*. New York: Clarion Books.

Analysis Guide: Wordless Picturebook

Approaching the Wordless Picturebook

- Pick up the picturebook, attending to the size, format (horizontal or vertical), materials used in construction of book (papers, graphics).
- Consider the author-illustrator of the text. What media is used in the illustrations?
- Look at the cover, title, and illustrations. What expectations are set up for you as you approach the picturebook? What does the cover, title, and illustrations suggest?
- What is included in the peritext? The dedication, title page, author's note, summary statement, etc.
- Since there are no words, how are the illustrations sequenced? Are borders used to separate the images? What reading paths are suggested by the composition of the individual images?

Reading the Wordless Picturebook

- What were your initial reactions to the illustrations?
- What kind of gaps does the illustrator leave for the reader to fill in? What details are purposefully left out to create tension?
- How does the story flow from panel to panel or page to page?

Analyzing the Wordless Picturebook

- Consider the series of images in the picturebook. Do the images change over the course of the book? Do they get bigger, smaller, change?
- How are borders and image gutters used in the narrative?
- How much time elapses or settings change in between the images in the narrative sequence?

Further Resources

Crawford, P. A., & Hade, D. (2000). Inside the picture, outside the frame: Semiotics and the reading of wordless picture books. *Journal of Research in Childhood Education, 15*(1), 66–80.

Doonan, J. (1993). *Looking at pictures in picture books*. Stroud, UK: Thimble Press.

Graham, J. (1990). *Pictures on the page*. Exeter, UK: Short Run Press.

Kiefer, B. (1995). *The potential of picturebooks: From visual literacy to aesthetic understanding*. Englewood Cliffs, NJ: Prentice-Hall.

Meek, M. (1988). *How texts teach what readers learn*. Stroud, UK: Thimble Press.

Pantaleo, S. (2007). "How could that be?" Reading Banyai's *Zoom* and *Re-Zoom*. *Language Arts, 84*(3), 222–233.

Pantaleo, S. (2008). The framed and the framing in *Flotsam*. *Journal of Children's Literature, 34*(1), 22–29.

Exploring Historical Fiction Picturebooks

Central Focus of the Unit

Historical fiction, as the name implies, blends actual historical characters and events with fictionalized or composite characters to present a compelling portrayal of the past. Details of everyday life and factual accounts of the times and settings portrayed propel the reader back in time to make the past come to life in this genre. Historical fiction must not only be an accurate rendition of historical events, it must also be a quality narrative. In this genre, fictional plot structures and the perspectives of marginalized groups are often used to construct a narrative centered on actual historical events.

The blending of fact and fiction and attention to which events, settings, characters, and perspectives are accurate portrayals and which are constructed, are an important consideration in understanding the fictional nature of this genre. In general, the setting is historically accurate and the characters are a blend of real and fictionalized people. Having students understand which characters are real and which have been created is an important consideration with historical fiction picturebooks.

All historical accounts are portrayed from a particular perspective, and understanding the diversity of perspectives is as important as understanding the portrayal offered. Reading more than one version of a particular event is a good way for students to see the constructed nature of these stories and to begin to analyze the ways individual stories present historical information from a variety of points of view. It is as important to understand the perspective of a historical account, as it is to understand the actual account.

Cornerstone Text or Visual Image

Henry's Freedom Box (Levine, 2007) tells the story of a slave named Henry Brown and his harrowing journey to escape slavery during the Civil War era. Henry builds a box and hides himself in it and sends it to Philadelphia as a means of escaping a slave plantation in Virginia. The story is told through the eyes of Henry Brown as he endures the hardships associated with his journey to freedom.

Learning Objectives

- Understand the characteristics of historical fiction picturebooks as a genre.
- Analyze the tension created between historical accuracy and fictional narrative elements of historical fiction picturebooks.
- Navigate and analyze the visual elements of historical fiction picturebooks, including: peritextual elements, font, borders, composition, illustration techniques, visual metaphor, and artistic style.
- Understand the point of view of the author and illustrator in historical fiction picturebooks and how this perspective affects the story.
- Analyze the way images are constructed and how these constructions affect the meaning potentials of individual images in historical fiction picturebooks.

Launching the Unit

This unit begins with the reading and analysis of one particular picturebook, for example, *Henry's Freedom Box*, to help students understand the complexities involved in blending historical facts and fictionalized elements. The past is portrayed in historical fiction picturebooks through visual images, design elements, and written narrative. How each of these elements adds to students' understandings of historical events and themes is an important focus in this unit.

Throughout *Henry's Freedom Box*, the illustrator, Kadir Nelson, draws on historical research to ensure accuracy in the representation of the characters, settings, and objects depicted. For example, on the water pitcher placed on a table in one illustration, the pitcher features a drawing of a Black slave from the antislavery movement with the quote "Am I Not a Man and a Brother?" positioned below the image. Calling students' attention to these visual images and helping them interpret these visual symbols that relate to the theme of the picturebook expands the meaning potentials of this genre.

In addition, an important aspect of reading historical fiction is attending to the peritext for information contained in author and illustrator notes, further information placards, and associated online resources. Determining the historical accuracy of particular objects, settings, characters, or events is done through comparing and contrasting various sources of information and using these comparisons to weigh the information presented. Internet searches, author-illustrator websites, historical references, and other reference material for historical information are important resources for unlocking the potential of historical fiction picturebooks.

Lessons and Learning Experiences

1. *Visual Clues to the Past*—For many years, access to many of the images that are part of the Library of Congress image bank was unavailable.

Recently, the Library of Congress and many important museums have provided royalty-free access to many of the pieces of art, photographs, and memorabilia of historical eras. These images are often used by artists in the creation of their illustrations for historical fiction picturebooks. Looking at the primary source versions of these images is an important way of understanding the perspectives and artistic techniques employed by the illustrator. Conduct a *think-aloud* in front of your students, by describing what you are thinking about as you analyze an image from a picturebook. The focus is on *how* you think through an image, not necessarily *what* you are thinking about. Practice describing the image by yourself before trying this in front of students.

2. *Three-Level Analysis of an Image*—An analytical framework was described in detail in Part II of this book that involved three levels of analysis. In that framework, students were asked to consider a visual image from perceptual, structural, and ideological perspectives. In this lesson, we ask students to consider a single image, or series of images, from these three perspectives. Using a three-column chart with the following headings may be helpful:

   • What Do You Notice? (Perceptual)
   • How Is the Image Constructed? (Structural)
   • From Whose Point of View Is the Image Portrayed? (Ideological)

3. *Point of View*—It is important to consider from whose perspective a story is being portrayed. Identifying the narrative perspective as first person or third person is a good place to begin. Not only should we be concerned with the narrative perspective, but the perspective from which the images are portrayed. Is the student viewing the scene from eye level, above, or below the perspectives of the characters? Is the viewer able to see things the characters cannot see? How does the visual perspective emphasize some elements and not others?

4. *Fictional versus Factual Elements*—When reading historical fiction we often ask ourselves: Is this true? How much of this is true? How can we distinguish fact from fiction? These are important considerations when reading historical fiction. An important lesson during this unit is a discussion on what historical facts are presented, from whose perspective are these offered, and what evidence for determining the accuracy of the historical portrayal, or the fictionalized nature of the visual and textual information is available. We can help students consider various elements of the picturebook and discuss whether they are factual or fictional by analyzing the portrayals of characters, settings, and events as either factual or fictional.

5. *Four Questions*—Using sticky notes or a sheet of paper divided into quarters, have students consider the following four questions as they read a historical fiction picturebook:

a.   How does the main character change in the course of the book?
b.   Is there anything missing from the story that should have been addressed?
c.   Did anything surprise you as you read through this book?
d.   Did anything confuse you about the story?

There is nothing magical about the number four, or the questions I have suggested here. This learning experience focuses students' attention on particular aspects of historical fiction picturebooks and features four questions that have worked to generate effective discussions.

Culminating Projects

One possible project would be to have students write and illustrate a historical fiction picturebook. Other possibilities would be to incorporate historical events and information into other multimodal ensembles, for example brochures, museum exhibits, posters, political cartoons, journals, or newspaper accounts. Using visual images and written language to present one's understandings of historical events is an important part of this culminating experience.

Text Set

Bradby, M. (1995). *More than anything else*. New York: Orchard.
Bunting, E. (1990). *The wall*. New York: Clarion Books.
Bunting, E. (1996). *Train to somewhere*. New York: Scholastic.
Bunting, E. (1998). *So far from the sea*. New York: Houghton Mifflin.
Coles, R. (1995). *The story of Ruby Bridges*. New York Scholastic.
Innocenti, R. (1985). *Rose Blanche*. New York: Creative Paperbacks.
Levine, E. (2007). *Henry's freedom box*. New York: Scholastic.
Mochizuki, K. (1993). *Baseball saved us*. New York: Lee & Low.
Munoz Ryan, P. (1999). *Amelia and Eleanor go for a ride*. New York: Scholastic.
Munoz Ryan, P. (2002). *When Marian sang*. New York: Scholastic.
Polacco, P. (1994). *Pink and say*. New York: Philomel Books.
Polacco, P. (2000). *The butterfly*. New York: Philomel Books.
Ringgold, F. (1992). *Aunt Harriet's underground railroad in the sky*. New York: Scholastic.
Say, A. (2002). *Home of the brave*. New York: Houghton Mifflin.
Tsuchiya, Y. (1988). *Faithful elephants: A true story of animals, people and war*. New York: Houghton Mifflin.
Turner, A. (1987). *Nettie's trip south*. New York: Aladdin Paperbacks.
Turner, A. (1992). *Katie's trunk*. New York: Aladdin.
Wild, M. (1991). *Let the celebrations begin!* New York: Orchard Books.
Yolen, J. (1992). *Encounter*. San Diego: Harcourt Brace.

Analysis Guide: Historical Fiction

Historical Elements:

- Has the book focused on a popular historical event?
- What background and contextual knowledge is necessary for understanding this particular era or historical event?
- Has a particular historical period been accurately portrayed? Are there any errors in setting, plot, or the time sequence?
- Are there any anomalous elements in the visual images (things out of place)?
- Are there are visual motifs or metaphors that have been used in the images?
- Does the setting contain accurate information? Places? Geographical information? How is the setting illustrated?
- Does the description of the setting fit the historical period? Do the images of characters' clothing look accurate?
- Are there real historical figures whose names you recognize?
- Are the historical characters accurately portrayed?

Fictional Elements:

- What aspects of the story have been fictionalized?
- Are the fictionalized characters believable? If so, in what ways?
- What is the author trying to say about the historical period?
- Is the author revealing any new insights about the historical characters or historical events?
- What comment do you think the author is making about this social conditions of the time portrayed?
- Are there any visual elements that add to the theme or message being offered?
- From whose perspective is the story being told? How does this affect the way the story is told?
- Are there other perspectives on the events available? How would the story change if told from a different perspective?
- Who has been excluded from the story? How might this change the story?

Peritextual Elements:

- What do you notice on the cover of the picturebook?
- What are the most important features on the cover?
- What is the title of the book? What does this title mean to you?

- Has the book garnered any awards displayed on the cover?
- What colors dominate the cover design?
- What is in the foreground? What is in the background? What is the significance of these placements?
- Are any characters represented on the cover?
- Is the character looking at you? How does this affect you?
- Is the character looking away or at someone or something else? How does this affect you?
- What do you notice about the endpages?
- Do the endpages contain a visual narrative?
- Do the endpages contribute to the visual continuity of the picturebook?
- What information is contained in the front and back book jacket?
- How does the jacket information help to establish background information for the story? How does this information help you to understand the story?
- What clues are given about the facts being presented?

Further Resources

Beck, C., Nelson-Faulkner, S., & Mitchell-Pierce, K. (2000). Historical fiction: Teaching tool or literary experience. *Language Arts, 77*(6), 546–555.

Scott O'Dell Award for Historical Fiction available at http://www.scottodell.com/pages/ScottO'DellAwardforHistoricalFiction.aspx

Serafini, F. (2008). Approaching, navigating and comprehending picturebooks. *WSRA: Journal of the Wisconsin State Reading Association. 47*(2), 5–9.

Serafini, F. (2010). Expository fiction: Blurring the boundaries between fiction and non-fiction in *Dragonology* and *The Discovery of Dragons. The Journal of Children's Literature.* 36(1), 28–34.

Tally, B., & Goldenberg, L. B. (2005). Fostering historical thinking with digitized primary sources. *Journal of Research on Technology in Education, 38*(1), 1–21.

Youngs, S. (2012). Understanding history through the visual images in historical fiction. *Language Arts, 89*(6), 379–395.

Youngs, S., & Serafini, F. (2011). Comprehension strategies for reading historical fiction picturebooks. *The Reading Teacher.* International Reading Association. *65*(2), 115–124.

Exploring Informational Picturebooks

Central Focus of the Unit

Informational picturebooks, also known as expository texts, are used extensively throughout elementary and middle grade classrooms to help students find infor mation about the world around them, conduct research into specific content area topics, and expose students to a type of reading other than fictional narrative. I choose the term *informational text* rather than nonfiction because it is associated with the purpose of the text rather than its inherent truth value.

An extensive array of informational picturebooks is available for introducing students to any number of content area topics. From anacondas to zebras, infor-mational picturebooks can be used to develop students' sense of curiosity about the natural world, explore topics of interest, learn about scientific discoveries, and come to understand and appreciate other people and places.

Some of the challenges students have with informational texts are the differ-ent structures and features they encounter in them, the background knowledge necessary for making sense of their topics, and the vocabulary used in these texts. In order to overcome these challenges, teachers need to demonstrate how these texts are read and used; call students' attention to the visual, textual, and design el-ements of these texts; and teach students how to comprehend the various written structures that accompany the visual components of these multimodal ensembles.

Informational picturebooks are an endangered genre in children's publishing due to the vast amounts of information available for free through online resources. In a competition based solely on the amount of information presented, informa-tional picturebooks will surely become obsolete. Therefore, print-based, informa-tional picturebooks often incorporate a hook or gimmick to remain viable. From crop and reveal formats, those formats where readers see a small portion of an image and are invited to guess what it might be that allow suspense and predic-tion to play a role in the act of reading, to blended narrative and informational structures like the use of fictional story lines in the popular *Magic School Bus* series, the informational picturebook draws on multiple features and structures to deliver information and catch the interest of young readers.

Cornerstone Text or Visual Image

For this unit of study, I have selected one of my own picturebooks, entitled *Looking Closely Along the Shore* (Serafini, 2008a), as a cornerstone text. Because I have extensive information about the creation of these texts, I might use this picturebook as a way to provide an insider's perspective on the creation and use of informational picturebooks. *Looking Closely Along the Shore* is an informational picturebook about the natural habitat and creatures that live along the shorelines across North America. This book is one in a series of six books that focus on a variety of biomes or natural habitats. Utilizing a crop and reveal format, this book uses nature photography to draw students' attention to the creatures and objects one may find along the shore.

In addition, I would recommend any of the *Eyewitness* series by DK Publishing. These texts incorporate beautiful illustrations and photographs with informative captions and expository writing. There are so many wonderful informational texts to choose from that I suggest teachers use whatever texts they find most informative and of superior quality.

Learning Objectives

- Help students understand the different ways information can be presented in informational texts, including design elements, written language, and photography.
- Create a list of essential criteria for analyzing the elements, features, and writing style of informational texts.
- Develop strategies for making sense of the various visual, textual, and design components of informational texts.
- Learn how various elements of informational picturebooks work, and use these elements in one's own research reports and projects.
- Develop students' abilities to discern between fact and opinion, theories and evidence, and to understand how an author's perspective plays a role in the information presented.

Launching the Unit

In order to get students to attend to the variety of features in informational texts, I have used a *scavenger hunt activity* to get students to generate an extensive inventory of all the features and structures they can find in the books we are exploring. A list of the features students might encounter includes:

- Charts and Graphs
- Diagrams
- Maps

- Concept Maps
- Glossary
- Table of Contents
- Photographs
- Illustrations
- Captions
- Headings and Sub-Headings
- Index

From this list, teachers will need to decide which features to address and share strategies for interpreting them. Next, teachers will need to find quality examples to demonstrate what these features look like, and more important, what they can do for the student. Understanding the function of these features helps students make connections to their own writing when they are asked to create research papers and projects by themselves. This activity begins with how these features are used by readers and continues with understanding how to use them as writers and designers.

When I was preparing my picturebooks for publication, I was unaware of the importance of design decisions in the publishing process. I mistakenly did not concern myself with how the gutter would fall across particular images, the way fonts are used in informational texts, and the use of different writing structures for conveying information to young readers in such a limited amount of space. These experiences have helped me focus students' attention on the design elements of informational texts, for example fonts, frames, headings, and layout. It is not simply the quality of the writing or the visual images that make an informational text effective; often, it is the effectiveness of the design and organization of the material that supports young readers.

After students have generated an inventory of informational text features, teachers may select and demonstrate one feature at a time using examples from the texts students explored. Basically, the list becomes a curriculum guide for exposing students to informational texts. Spend time with the features students encounter the most, the ones they struggle with, and the ones they most likely would adopt for use in their own writing and designs.

Lessons and Learning Experiences

1. *Choosing Informational Books*—One of the ongoing lessons in this unit of study is to help students develop criteria for evaluating the effectiveness and quality of various informational texts. I introduce students to the following criteria for selecting high-quality informational picturebooks: accuracy of information, authority of authors, organization of material, quality of visual images and design, quality of written text, and the inclusion of references to the sources used in the book's creation.

The criteria we will use to evaluate these texts will evolve as students' understandings of these texts evolves.

2. *Reading Images in Informational Texts*—Using the grammars of visual design presented in Chapter 5 of this book, I demonstrate to students how to approach, navigate, and analyze various images in the books they are reading. I discuss with students concepts like information zones, modality, salience, and framing. Teaching students to focus on *how* images are composed and presented is just as important as *what* is presented. For example, I would collect various images of wolves that come from both fictional and informational texts. Showing students cartoons, pencil drawings, and photographs of wolves and asking them to discuss which one seems the most real is a good way to address the concept of modality.

3. *Informational Text Award Committee*—The Robert F. Sibert Medal from the American Library Association and the Orbis Pictus Award from the National Council Teachers of English are medals awarded to the most distinguished informational texts each year. On their websites you can find the criteria they use to determine the winners. Using these criteria, have students serve on a classroom-based committee that selects an informational text from the classroom library to receive their "best informational text" award. The focus of this experience is to help students understand and apply the criteria of high-quality informational texts to the books they have been exploring.

4. *Visual Image Think-Aloud*—Select a single visual image associated with a content area topic that you have chosen to explore. In front of the class, *think aloud* about how you would approach, navigate, and analyze the selected image. Use the vocabulary of visual composition introduced in this book to describe what you are attending to. The focus of this lesson is to demonstrate how to talk about a single image, and how to help students analyze the visual composition and content of the images they will encounter.

5. *Representation Across Modes*—Select a particular concept or piece of evidence, for example the life cycle, and demonstrate the various ways this information can be represented. Compare and contrast a life cycle diagram, video clip, written description, model, or series of photographs. Help students discuss the affordances and limitations of each mode of representation and how they might use each mode in their own projects and presentations.

Culminating Projects

Two of the most common culminating projects for informational texts used in schools are the science fair project and the research paper. Working from a visual literacies perspective, we need to expand the tools and resources students are allowed to use to represent and share what they have learned. Allow students to use PowerPoint, Prezi, video clips, photography, writing, models, building blocks, or websites to present and share what they have been studying and have learned. Don't let the creation of these projects get in the way or overshadow the value in the explorations and analyses of the informational texts read across this unit.

Text Set

This text set is more difficult to specify because of the enormous amount of informational texts currently available. Instead, I will list some of my favorite series and authors of informational texts, and have listed below links to the two most prominent awards in informational text publishing.

Some Favorite Authors of Informational Texts:

Aliki
George Ancona
Seymour Simon
Gail Gibbons
Lois Ehlert
David Adler
Jerry Palotta
Ruth Heller
David Macauley
Jim Arnosky
Leonard Everett Fisher
Diane Stanley
James Cross Giblin
Russell Freedman

Additional Resources

Assorted books from the *Eyewitness Series* by DK Publishing.
Serafini, F. (2008a). *Looking closely along the shore*. Toronto, Canada: Kids Can Press.
Serafini, F. (2008b). *Looking closely through the forest*. Toronto, Canada: Kids Can Press.
Serafini, F. (2008c). *Looking closely across the desert*. Toronto, Canada: Kid Can Press.
Serafini, F. (2008d). *Looking closely inside the garden*. Toronto, Canada: Kid Can Press.
Serafini, F. (2010a). *Looking closely into the rainforest*. Toronto, Canada: Kids Can Press.
Serafini, F. (2010b). *Looking closely around the pond*. Toronto, Canada: Kids Can Press.

Analysis Guide: Informational Texts

Content:

- Is the information up to date?
- Is the information accurate?

- Is the information relevant to the reader?
- Were authentic or primary sources used?
- What are the author's qualifications?

Writing/Style:

- Is the text easily read and followed?
- Were stereotypes avoided?
- Were multiple points of view or perspectives used?

Organization:

- Were text features used effectively?
- Do the table of contents, headings, index, glossary, and sidebars help present the information?
- Does the structural layout and page composition support the content?

Quality of Graphic Elements:

- Were quality photographs, illustrations, diagrams, maps, figures, or graphs used to present content?
- Were the captions helpful and well organized?
- Were any primary source materials used?

Critical Analysis:

- Does the information presented here fit with other books on the subject?
- What are the qualifications of the author or illustrator to present this content?
- What are the tensions concerning concepts and evidence in this field of inquiry?

Further Resources

Colman, P. (2007). A new way to look at literature: A visual model for analyzing fiction and nonfiction texts. *Language Arts, 84*(3), 257–268.

Gill, S. R. (2009). What teachers need to know about the "new" nonfiction. *The Reading Teacher, 63*(4), 260–267.

Harvey, S. (1998). *Nonfiction matters: Reading, writing, and research in grades 3–8.* York, ME: Stenhouse.

Hoyt, L. (2002). *Make it real: Strategies for success with informational texts.* Portsmouth, NH: Heinemann

Hoyt, L., Mooney, M., & Parkes, B. (Eds.). (2003). *Exploring informational texts: From theory to practice.* Portsmouth, NH: Heinemann.

Moss, B. (2003). *Exploring the literature of fact: Children's nonfiction trade books in the elementary classroom.* New York: Guilford Press.

NCTE Orbis Pictus Award for Outstanding Nonfiction for Children available at http://www.ncte.org/awards/orbispictus

Pappas, C. (1991). Fostering full access to literacy by including information books. *Language Arts, 68*, 449–462.

Portalupi, J., & Fletcher, R. (2001). *Nonfiction craft lessons: Teaching information writing K–8*. Portland, ME: Stenhouse.

Robert F. Sibert Informational Book Medal available at http://www.ala.org/alsc/awardsgrants/bookmedia/sibertmedal

Saul, E. W., & Dieckman, D. (2005). Choosing and using information trade books. *Reading Research Quarterly, 40*(4), 502–513.

Exploring Illustrated Novels

Central Focus of the Unit

This unit of study focuses on the vast array of *illustrated novels* that are available today, most of which have been published in the past 20 years. Under this umbrella term, I include a range of contemporary novels that draw upon varying amounts of illustrations in their presentation. In this particular unit, I will focus on longer works of fiction (novels) that include illustrations and save comics and graphic novels for the next unit of study. The novels I am referring to would range from those with minimal illustrations, like the *Harry Potter* series, in which only the chapter openings are illustrated, to novels that draw upon illustrations as an essential element in their presentation, like *The Invention of Hugo Cabret* and *Wonderstruck* by Brian Selznick (2007; 2011). In between these two ends of the continuum we find illustrations used in different ways to add to the presentation of the narrative.

Just as postmodern picturebooks feature images, the inclusion of visual images and graphic elements in contemporary novels signals postmodern influences on these texts, especially in addition to nonlinear structures, metafictive devices, and multiple narrators. The novels students encounter in and out of schools today incorporate visual elements as a prominent feature, and are not constrained by the conventions of written language and design as traditional novels used in schools.

In many contemporary novels, illustrations have been added to attract readers' attention and provide additional detail to the narrative rendered primarily in written language. The written narrative in some novels, like the books written by Roald Dahl and illustrated by Quentin Blake, could stand on its own without the accompanying illustrations. Other narratives, like the two novels by Brian Selznick mentioned above, would not make any sense without the accompanying illustrations. In fact, since *The Invention of Hugo Cabret* won the Caldecott Award, some educators consider it a picturebook. For my purposes, I would include it in the genre of illustrated novels because of the book's extended length (533 pages) and novel-like size, shape, and format.

A distinguishing feature of the illustrated novel, as compared to a picturebook, would be the length of the written narrative and the physical dimensions of the book itself. In general, illustrated novels are the same size as traditional novels, not larger formats like picturebooks. Another important consideration would be the role the illustrations play in rendering the narrative. In general, the images included in these novels play a subservient role to the written text, but as we move closer to the characteristics of Selznick's illustrated novels, such as *Wonderstruck*, the images play a more central role in the rendering of the narrative. I believe there are enough contemporary novels that include illustrations to varying degrees that illustrated novels warrant some exploration as a genre in and of itself.

Cornerstone Text or Visual Image

For this unit, I have selected a range of illustrated novels including *The Graveyard Book* (Gaiman, 2010), *Miss Peregrine's Home for Peculiar Children* (Riggs, 2011), *Making Up Megaboy* (Walter, 1999), and *The Invention of Hugo Cabret* (Selznick, 2007). I have selected these novels and suggest introducing them in this particular order because they are purposefully ordered from those that use visual images as merely illustrative, in the case of *The Graveyard Book,* to those that depend more on the use of visual images, as in *The Invention of Hugo Cabret* to tell their stories. These selected cornerstone texts represent the wide range of roles that illustrations play in contemporary novels. *The Graveyard Book* includes black and white illustrations on some pages throughout the novel; however, its illustrations are primarily decorative in nature. The images included in *The Graveyard Book* and *Miss Peregrine's Home for Peculiar Children* illustrate events and characters that are also described in the written narrative. The illustrations in these texts do not add details of their own; rather they serve as traditional illustrative devices. The illustrations in Selznick's novel are more essential to the telling of the story, adding elements that are not depicted in the written narrative. Selznick reportedly wrote these books originally without any illustrations, and then afterward selected portions of the novels to take out and replace with illustrations that propelled the story forward in place of written language.

Miss Peregrine's Home for Peculiar Children is a novel illustrated with old photographs of children collected by the author from discarded family photo albums. This eerie novel uses manipulated photographs to depict the peculiar nature of the characters in the story. *Making Up Megaboy* (Walter, 1999) is a unique novel told from the point of view of multiple narrators about the shooting of a storeowner at a local bodega. The story is told from the point of view of the shooter, a news reporter, the shooter's teacher, a policeman, and the boy's mother. These four examples of illustrated novels represent a range of uses of visual images in contemporary novels and were selected to allow students to compare and contrast how visual images are used across these multimodal ensembles.

Learning Objectives

- Develop students' awareness of the various roles played by illustrations in contemporary novels.
- Support students' transition from reading picturebooks to engaging with longer works of fiction.
- Compare the rendering of narrative in visual formats to the details provided in written language.
- Develop a sense of the changes taking place in the literary and visual formats of contemporary novels.
- Demonstrate strategies for students to use to navigate and interpret illustrated novels.

Launching the Unit

Introducing the wide variety of uses for illustrations in contemporary novels is an appropriate starting point for this unit of study. Using the text set provided in this section, share with students the variety of ways illustrations are used. Invite students to find examples of illustrated novels on their own and create a chart or bulletin board outlining the different ways illustrations are used in contemporary novels. For me, rendering a continuum that runs from minimal use of images or images as illustrations, to the use of images as an essential element in the story might be a good way to demonstrate the wide range of uses.

Another important distinction to make with students is the difference between illustrated novels and comics or graphic novels. Developing a sense of the illustrated novel genre involves distinguishing it from other genres and formats. Discuss with students the features of illustrated novels and how they are similar and different from graphic novels and comic books.

After selecting one of the recommended cornerstone texts, work with students to demonstrate how to analyze the use of illustrations in a single text. I think *Making Up Megaboy* makes for an excellent analysis and discussion. Each of the different perspectives throughout this book is illustrated using different techniques and materials, Discuss why the author, illustrator, designer, and publisher might have selected the various techniques and materials. Ask students how each of the illustrations adds to or expands the narrative offered in this book.

Lessons and Learning Experiences

1. *Illustrating Written Language*—Since the focus of this unit is on the relationship between narrative descriptions in written language and how narratives are rendered through visual images, have students take a section of a novel and try illustrating what is presented in writing. Students should be allowed to select the section they would like to illustrate and use a variety of illustrative techniques and resources to

create their illustrations. There are many possible choices of material and interpretations. What is important is to have students discuss and defend why they made the choices they made.

2. *A Picture is Worth . . .*—As an alternative to the first learning experience, have students try using written language to describe the same aspects of a narrative that an illustration depicts. Of course, it will never be exactly the same thing since these two modes do things in different ways, but this lesson should help students understand how the two modes work in greater depth.

3. *Storyboarding*—Narratives are rendered in a variety of sequences, any of which would change the sense of the overall narrative. Have students take a chapter and envision what it might look like visually and then create a storyboard like filmmakers do to display the various scenes and actions throughout the narrative. Sketches are used to offer ideas, not fully completed drawings. Keep the focus on the story.

4. *Reading Without Images*—Take one of Brian Selznick's two illustrated novels and read a chapter aloud without revealing the images to students. Discuss what is missing and any confusion that might arise. What do the illustrations do for the reader in these texts? What do you miss out on when you do not attend to the illustrations?

5. *Author and Illustrator Websites*—Revealing the process by which these illustrated novels are created provides students with insights not available simply by reading these books. Many of the authors of illustrated novels, in particular Neil Gaiman and Brian Selznick, have built wonderfully informative and entertaining websites about how these books were conceived and created. Have students explore the various web-based resources and help them to use these resources to broaden their perspectives for interpreting these novels.

Culminating Projects

Like many of these units of study, the culminating projects should be seen as opportunities for students to engage with these texts as insiders. We invite students to select examples from novels they want to emulate and try to create some images for themselves. Have students take a piece of writing they have been working on and try rendering a few pages as an illustrated text. Making decisions about what to illustrate and what to leave as written text allows students to experience the same tough decisions published authors and illustrators make every day.

Text Sets

Alexie, S. (2007). *The absolutely true diary of a part-time Indian*. New York: Little Brown Young Readers.

Dahl, R. (1980). *The twits*. New York: Penguin.

Gaiman, N. (2010). *The graveyard book*. New York: HarperCollins.

Hawking, L., Hawking, S., & Parsons, G. (2009).*George's secret key to the universe*. New York: Simon & Schuster.

Holm, J., & Holm, M. (2005). *Babymouse: Queen of the world*. New York: Random House.

Kinney, J. (2007). *Diary of a wimpy kid*. New York: Amulet.

Mowll, J. (2005). *Operation Red Jericho*. New York: Random House.

Myers, W. D. (1999). *Monster*. New York: Harper Collins

Ness, P. (2011). *A monster calls: Inspired by an idea from Siobhan Dowd*. New York: Candlewick.

Pilkey, D. (1997). *The adventures of Captain Underpants*. New York: Blue Sky.

Riggs, R. (2011). *Miss Peregrine's home for peculiar children*. Philadelphia: Quirk Books.

Selznick, B. (2007). *The invention of Hugo Cabret*. New York: Scholastic.

Selznick, B. (2011). *Wonderstruck*. New York: Scholastic.

Walter, V. (1999). *Making up Megaboy*. New York: Delacorte.

Analysis Guides: Illustrated Novels

Cover and Peritextual Elements

- How is the title/subtitle presented? (color, size, position)
- How are the names of authors or illustrators presented?
- What design elements dominate the cover? (lines, shapes, color, borders)
- What are the characteristics of the fonts used?
- Are people included on the cover? If so, who is represented?
- What stands out on the cover? How is it made to stand out?
- What is being used as the hook? What compelled you to choose or not choose this book?

Interior Illustrations

- What visual media are utilized? (photograph, line art, collage, other)
- How do the illustrations relate to the written narrative? Do they add more information, or do they simply illustrate what has been written?
- How is the setting illustrated?
- How are characters portrayed? In what clothing? Doing what?
- What designs or objects are represented?
- Do the characters look at the viewer in any illustrations (demand) or away (offer)? What does this suggest?
- Are the images realistic or abstract?
- What has been left out of the illustrative process? What aspects of the narrative have not been illustrated? Why?

Further Resources

Appleman, D. (2000). *Critical encounters in high school English: Teaching literary theory to adolescents.* New York: Teachers College Press.

Callow, J. (1999). *Image matters: Visual texts in the classroom.* Marrickville, NSW: Primary English Teaching Association.

Eckert, L. S. (2006). *How does it mean?: Engaging reluctant readers through literary theory.* Portsmouth, NH: Heinemann.

Hassett, D. D., & Schieble, M. B. (2007). Finding space and time for the visual in K–12 literacy instruction. *English Journal, 97*(1), 62–68.

Serafini, F. (2011). Expanding perspectives for comprehending visual images in multimodal texts. *Journal of Adolescent and Adult Literacy. 54*(5), 342–350.

Serafini, F., & Blasingame, J. (2012). The changing face of the young adult novel. *The Reading Teacher, 66*(2), 145–148.

Exploring Graphic Novels, Comics, and Cartoons

Central Focus of the Unit

The number of graphic novels, comics, and cartoons published in the past 10 years has increased dramatically. Unfortunately, comic books, cartoons, and graphic novels have not been as welcome in the traditional curriculum as picturebooks and other multimodal ensembles. Often viewed as simplistic or as low status texts, these pulp narratives are a favorite among young readers outside of school, especially boys. Although girls have taken up graphic novels in earnest in recent years, the readers of comics and graphic novels are still primarily boys. Superheroes, violence, fantastical and supernatural elements, and action-based plots are the features of the graphic novels and comics that often attract boys.

Eisner (2008) described graphic novels and comics as a type of *sequential art*. McCloud (1994) asserted that comics are pictorial images juxtaposed with written text in sequential form intended to convey an aesthetic response in the reader-viewer. These definitions point to the multimodal nature of graphic novels, comics, and cartoons utilizing visual, textual, and design elements in their presentation. They also suggest these texts are both a narrative form and a visual art form. To understand graphic novels, comics, and cartoons, students have to develop strategies for dealing with the narrative, design, and visual elements of these multimodal texts.

In addition, graphic novels, comic books, comic strips, and cartoons are identified by the use of panels and gutters. *Panels* are the sequential boxes containing the illustrations and written text that comprise a comic book or graphic novel. The *gutter* is the space between the panels. In a comic that uses one image, sometimes referred to as a cartoon, there are no gutters. Comic strips are published in newspapers and magazines on a regular basis and are usually comprised of three to five panels at a time. Many graphic novels are simply bound versions of individual comic books. However, more and more graphic novels are now initially published as novel-length, visual narratives.

The majority of graphic novels are science fiction or fantasy. Like comics books, graphic novels often feature supernatural and fantastical elements, for example superheroes saving the world and otherworldly creatures roaming imaginary lands. *Manga*, which means "amusing drawings," is a popular Japanese form of graphic novel that includes indirect, nonlinear plots and imaginary worlds intended for young adult readers. Although manga is read from the back of the book to the front and from right to left, many of the same structures and visual designs are incorporated into these graphic novels.

Political cartoons are another genre that could be explored in this unit. Although they often require a knowledge of politics and current events that students may not have yet acquired in order to be understood, they are a ubiquitous form of entertainment and satire that is easily found in newspapers and magazines, and are often quite humorous. Single panel cartoons are also a subgenre worthy of exploration in this unit. Many of these can be found daily in regional and nationally distributed newspapers. It might just be time to bring the funny papers into our classrooms!

This unit focuses on the variety of visual, textual, and design elements that are used in the creation of graphic novels, comics, and cartoons. As students develop an understanding of the features and organization of graphic novels, comics, and cartoons, they become more comfortable with these multimodal ensembles and develop their personal favorites.

Cornerstone Text or Visual Image

For the cornerstone texts for this unit, I suggest using a classic graphic novel like the Pulitzer Prize–winning *Maus I: A Survivor's Tale* (Spiegelman, 1986) and a contemporary set of graphic novels like the *Bone* series (Smith, 2005). *Maus* is an allegorical graphic novel depicting the atrocities of the Holocaust. The *Bone* series is a humorous, dark fantasy adventure revolving about three cousins, Phoney, Smiley, and Fone Bone, and their adventures that begin in the fictional town of Boneville. In addition to these graphic novels, I would add some examples of comic books and strips, and some single panel cartoons. The extensive variety of these texts provides opportunities for exploring many types of graphic novels, comics, and cartoons. Each of these subgenres could also be done as a separate unit.

Learning Objectives

- Develop a sense of the various features (panels, gutters, and narrative boxes) used in graphic novels, comics, and cartoons.
- Understand the syntactic rules and structures for reading graphic novels, comics, and cartoons.
- Help students understand how narratives are portrayed in visual formats.
- Demonstrate the various uses of the gutter in graphic novels and comics and how to infer from the gaps left in these visual spaces.
- Have students explore a range of graphic novels, manga, comics, and cartoons and understand the differences across these genres.

Launching the Unit

Although many students already have experience reading graphic novels, as in all the units of study, the process of exposing students to a wide variety of texts and images within a genre helps them understand what encompasses a particular genre or the focus of a unit, and begin to define what that genre entails. Because of the relatively shorter length of comics and graphic novels, students can experience a wide range of them in a short period of time. Bringing in traditional and new comic books series, collecting cartoons and comic strips from newspapers and magazines, and visiting the websites of Scott McCloud, the Eisner Comic Industry Awards, and others helps students see the range and variety of these multimodal ensembles.

I would continue by discussing the various techniques and features of graphic novels, comics, and cartoons. The following are some of the essential features of graphic novels and comics that students need to consider as they explore these texts:

- Panels—individual frames in a narrative sequence.
- The Gutter—the white space between panels used to transition between scenes, narrators, and time.
- Speech Bubbles—enclosed shapes used to depict thoughts or dialogue.
- Narrative Boxes—usually square or rectangular boxes at the top or bottom of a panel used to describe the setting, changes in time, or changes in narrators.
- Lettering & Punctuation—used to create moods, suggest verbal phrasing or intonation, as in all CAPITAL letters, and organize the textual elements.
- Benday Dots—the backgrounds used in varying degrees of density for shading and visual effects.

One of the challenges with this unit of study may be the lack of experience teachers have with these types of texts. For many older teachers, comic books were never allowed in school for reading pleasure, certainly not as required texts. We have to move past our own biases to be sure we incorporate the texts that students are reading outside of school, and provide them with the strategies they will need for making sense of the visual images and multimodal ensembles they encounter in and outside of school. Students need relevant experiences in school that connect them to the experiences they have with written narratives and visual images outside of school.

Lessons and Learning Experiences

1. *Understanding the Gutter*—The gutter is an important feature used in graphic novels and comics to transition across time, perspectives,

and settings. There are five transitions typically used in graphic novels and comics listed below. After gathering examples of each of these transitions, have students explore and discuss how the different transitions are used to propel the narrative forward in a comic book or graphic novel. The five transitions easily identified in comic books and graphic novels are:

- Moment to moment—time passing in same scene
- Action to action—actions in one or more scenes
- Subject to subject—characters change in same scene
- Scene to scene—changes in setting
- Aspect to aspect (of same scene)—changes in perspective

2. *Storyboarding Two Panels*—To help students better understand how transitions are accomplished by the gutter, have them create two illustrated panels and describe the relationship or transition between the two. Students can use the gutter to change scenes, perspectives, characters, or time. Each of these transitions changes the relationship among sequential panels and moves the narrative forward in different ways. Another way to do this would be to have students add a panel to an existing comic strip or graphic novel. Have them select an existing comic strip and add an additional panel to the strip suggesting what might occur in the next scene.

3. *Generating Captions*—In the back of *The New Yorker* magazine a contest is offered each week for readers to write a humorous caption to go with a cartoon draw by a staff cartoonist. Three entries are selected that represent different interpretations of the cartoon., A winner is selected by readers, and in addition to having his or her caption published with the cartoon, the winner receives a signed print of the cartoon. Have students try to write a funny caption to go with some of the cartoons in each week's edition and possibly submit them for publication to the magazine.

4. *Exploring Text Boxes*—In addition to the dialogue and thoughts presented in bubbles throughout various comics and graphic novels, written text in text boxes explains the transitions across time, setting, and narrator. At times, these text boxes are used to explain what has happened since the last panel, or to explain what is about to happen in the next panel. Have students explore the various ways that text boxes are used in graphic novels and comics.

5. *Letter Forms, Punctuation, and Onomatopoeia*—Individual words and symbols are frequently used in comics and graphic novels to express particular emotions or thoughts. In most superhero comic series, phrases like *Pow!* and *Bam!* are set apart by bubbles and other framing devices. The use of onomatopoeia helps express emotions in quick and short

phrases. Have students use these graphic elements to express feelings, thoughts, and actions in their own comic panels. In addition, how words are presented and how symbols are used in these texts is unique to this genre. Having students explore these features of the written text is as important as interpreting the visual features of graphic novels, comics, and cartoons.

Culminating Projects

Having students create single cartoons or comic strips is a wonderful project that students tend to engage with deeply. After exploring how various techniques and features are used, it makes sense for students to try them on their own. You could enlist the help of the art teacher to coordinate this project with what is happening in art class. Class books of student-made comics are great class projects.

Another project would be to invite a local cartoonist into the classroom to share her techniques and visual art forms. Students need to see that this form of visual art is read by people all over the world, and has been used for entertainment as well as for political satire.

Text Set

For this text set, I will share some of my favorite series and syndicated comics in addition to single titles.

Bone Series
Rockjaw Series
Watchmen Series
Sandman Series
Amulet Series
V for Vendetta
Maus—The Complete Maus
Hellboy
Marvel Comics—Batman, Superman, Spider-Man, Avengers, Fantastic
     Four, and many others
Peanuts Comics
Family Circle
The Far Side
Garfield
Calvin and Hobbes
Bloom County

Analysis Guide: Graphic Novels, Comics, and Cartoons

Graphic/Visual Convention	What Is It?	How Is It Used?
Speech Bubbles		
Thought Bubbles		
Narrative Boxes		
Letter Forms		
Panels		
Gutters		
Onomatopoeia		
Titles		

Further Resources

Bitz, M. (2010). *When commas meet kryptonite: Classroom lessons from the comic book project.* New York: Teachers College Press.

Cary, S. (2004). *Going graphic: Comics at work in the multilingual classroom.* Portsmouth, NH: Heinemann.

Center for Cartoon Studies: http://www.teachingcomics.org

Eisner Awards: http://www.eisnerawards.org

Eisner, W. (2008). *Comics and sequential art: Principles and practices from the legendary cartoonist Will Eisner.* New York: W. W. Norton.

Frey, N., & Fisher, D. (Eds.). (2008). *Teaching visual literacy: Using comic books, graphic novels, anime, cartoons, and more to develop comprehension and thinking skills.* Thousand Oaks, CA: Corwin Press.

Harvey Awards: http://www.harveyawards.org

Low, D. E. (2012). "Spaces invested with content": Crossing the "gaps" in comics with readers in schools. *Children's Literature in Education, 43*, 368–385.

McCloud, S. (1994). *Understanding comics: The invisible art.* New York: Harper.

Stafford, T. (2011). *Teaching visual literacy in the primary classroom: Comic books, film, television and picture narratives.* London: Routledge.

Thompson, T. (2008). *Adventures in graphica: Using comics and graphic novels to teach comprehension, 2–6.* York, ME: Stenhouse.

Yang, G. (2008). Graphic novels in the classroom. *Language Arts, 85*(3), 185–192.

Exploring Advertisements

Central Focus of the Unit

Along with news reports, documentaries, and web-based media, advertisements are an important area of concentration in media literacy educational frameworks. Advertisements are ubiquitous. It would be hard to imagine an ordinary day where we are not confronted by some form of advertisement in some context. Television, radio, newspapers, billboards, magazines, websites, and brochures all contain ads. In fact, most of the media outlets we enjoy rely on advertising dollars as their primary source of revenue.

The basic purpose of an advertisement is to persuade someone to do something, most often to purchase an object or a service being offered by a manufacturer or service provider. This persuasion can take many different forms, and can use many different techniques, ranging from testimonials to corporate branding, to accomplish these objectives. Advertisers craft their messages using a variety of visual elements and rhetorical devices to influence an audience's response. Crafting a coherent and persuasive visual argument or message is an important goal of most advertising campaigns. To do so, advertisers draw on visual images and design elements to connect people to particular products, offer testimonials on the product's behalf, or provide evidence of a product's value. Viewers of these advertisements make connections from the images presented to previous experiences, conjuring up both positive and negative emotions. Advertisers craft their messages based on anticipated responses from their targeted audiences, taking into account cultural norms, conventions, and histories.

Whether we object to advertising that targets younger and younger audiences directly, or we find the claims of particular products misleading, we have to accept the tremendous effect advertising has on our students. By the time our students start school, they have already been inundated with advertisements and exposed to media in many different forms. The purpose of this unit is not to hide students from the messages being offered, but rather to make them more skeptical of the messages they receive, and help them to analyze the ways in which advertisements appeal to their desires and connect with their identities when trying to get them to buy something. Helping students become critical consumers is a primary objective of media education.

Cornerstone Text or Visual Image

In general, any print or digital advertisement could provide a context for launching this unit of study. The advertisements featured in magazines aimed at a younger audience would provide students with opportunities to discuss products they have seen. Collecting advertisements about the products that students use and desire from a variety of sources helps connect students to the learning experiences we offer, and makes our media literacy curriculum more relevant to the lives of our students.

Learning Objectives

- Develop techniques for recognizing and questioning stereotypical representations and claims in advertisements.
- Understand the roles that print and image play in making claims in advertisements.
- Understand how advertisements work, including evidentiary bases, claims, arguments, testimonials, and compositional techniques.
- Learn to question the claims made in an advertisement, and conduct research to test the evidence provided.
- Understand the various *hooks* used in advertisements to appeal to a particular market or audience.

Launching the Unit

To introduce this unit, we have to help students recognize how many advertisements they are exposed to each day. Gathering a vast array of advertisements for students to analyze and having students conduct an inventory of the types of advertisements they encounter is a good way to start. Have students keep track of all the advertisements they see in a day or for a full week. Use the lists they generate as a way to get a sense of the types of advertisements and products your students care about and pay attention to. Categorize these lists of ads by the types of products being advertised, the media used, the context of the ad, and the types of visual elements used. Have students create a chart that incorporates the following categories:

- Product name
- Targeted audience
- Media type
- Context of reception
- Visual elements used
- Distribution outlet

After students have begun to realize how much their lives are inundated with advertisements, exploring how these advertisements work is essential. Drawing on the resources presented in the chapters on art, design, and visual grammar included in the first part of this book, help students analyze how an individual advertisement works. Discussing concepts like salience, information zones, framing, color, typography, and modality can help students unpack how particular advertisements present and distort their messages. For example, the concept of information zones suggests that information presented on the left side of a page or image represents the past, and the zone on the right represents the new or future. This concept relates to how advertisers use *before and after* photographs in their advertisements, with the before image on the left side of the advertisement and the after image on the right. It would look really weird to see it in the reverse order. In this way, the aspects of visual grammar discussed in this book can be used to understand the structures used in advertisements, how visual images are incorporated in advertisements, and how these elements affect the messages presented and distributed.

Lessons and Learning Experiences

1. *Magazine Analysis*—Select a children's magazine that students like to read and do a content analysis of the products and services being advertised in it. Count how many advertisements there are offered in one edition. Keep track of what is being advertised and what advertisements dominate the magazine. Also, have students consider what is not being advertised and why this might be the case. Getting a better sense of *what* is being advertised sets the foundation for analyzing *how* various products are being advertised.

2. *Visual Analysis*—Deconstruct an advertisement using the various visual grammar techniques, for example salience, social distance, offer-demand, vectors, and information zones presented in Chapter 5. How does the advertisement work? What structures are being used in various advertisements and in what manner?

3. *Political Advertisements*—Gather a series of advertisements promoting and discrediting a particular candidate. Consider how people, objects, and places are featured in these ads using the following categories:

Bodies:

- Age—innocence, wisdom, youth, success
- Gender—tough versus caring
- Race—who likes/does what
- Body Style—slim, fat, hair
- Looks—hair, culture, time, clothes

Manner:

- Expressions—happy, sad, excited, etc.
- Eye Contact (offer/demand)
- Pose—seductive, confident

Activity:

- Touch—who touches whom
- Movement—active/passive
- Positional Communication—spatial arrangement, closeness, distance

Props/Setting:

- Props—glasses, drinks, toys, tools
- Settings—natural, exotic, everyday, fantastical

4. *Media Differences*—Select advertisements that are featured in different media that focus on the same product. How is the product offered in different media, for different audiences? How does a television advertisement for a particular product differ from a print advertisement or one on the Internet? Is the message different? Is there a different hook for the same product? How do different audiences affect the types of advertisements being offered? Are particular audiences being targeted in particular contexts?

5. *Television Commercials*—Have students keep track of all the advertisements that run during an episode of one of their favorite television shows. Keep track of what is being advertised, how the advertised message is crafted, what is the suggested appeal of the product, and how the advertisers are trying to get students to respond. Is the advertisement an emotional appeal or an intellectual one? What claims are being made about the product? Are the claims justified by the evidence? Why do you think the advertisement appeared during this particular show?

Culminating Projects

The two projects I think would be most beneficial in this unit of study would be to construct an analysis guide with your students for exploring advertisements across various formats and media, and having students use the techniques discussed above to create an advertising campaign for a service or product associated with the classroom. The process of creating an analysis guide is probably more important than the actual guide that ends up being created. It is through the discussions and analyses that take place that students learn to understand and critique the advertisements they encounter on their own.

Text Sets

Selecting a particular text set for this unit is difficult due to the ever-changing world of advertisements. Exploring the advertisements that students are frequently exposed to, in particular those that appear on television and the radio, on websites, and in magazines, and are associated with the products they use on a regular basis, is an important consideration. Gathering advertisements from a variety of media makes us realize just how pervasive advertising is in our culture, and helps students attend to how often these images and messages affect their behaviors.

Analysis Guide: Advertisements

Sites of Reception: Considering the context of the advertisement.

- Why is the ad located where it is? How did you come across the ad?
- What background knowledge might be necessary to understand the ad?
- Who do you think is the target audience for this ad?
- How was the ad distributed?

Site of the Advertisement Itself: Look at the ad in its entirety.

- What are your initial impressions of the ad?
- What do you notice first? What seems to stand out for you?
- What materials are used to create the ad? Paintings, photos, collage?

Portrayal

- Who is portrayed in the ad? Who is not portrayed?
- What are the various actors doing? Who is doing what to whom?
- Where are the actors placed in the ad? Top or bottom?
- Are the actors looking at each other, away from the audience, or at the audience? What does this suggest?

Basic Elements of Design

- Consider the colors used. What impressions do you get from the dominant colors? Is the image black and white? If so, why might these colors be used?
- Consider size and scale. Why are certain elements larger than others? What does position add to possible meanings of position, power, or control?

Framing/Composition

- Are the text or images bordered or framed? Do the frames suggest anything on their own? Are there thick borders or faded edges?
- How is text and image combined? Where is the text located?

- Are the images contextualized or in an abstract space? How is white space used?

Visual Grammar

- What is located on the left, right, or center? (old and new) What is on the top or bottom of the ad? (real & ideal)
- Are there any recurring patterns, symbols, or motifs in the images?
- What is the "reality value" or level of abstraction? Are the images lifelike or stick figures?
- Consider the "path" your eyes follow as you approach the image. What catches your eye first? Why is that element salient?
- What is the ad trying to get you to look at through leading lines, colors, contrast, gestures, lighting?
- What is in focus or out of focus? How does it affect what you notice and consider significant?

Further Resources

Alvermann, D. E., Moon, J. S., & Hagood, M. C. (1999). *Popular culture in the classroom: Teaching and researching critical media literacy.* Newark, DE: International Reading Association.

Buckingham, D. (2003). *Media education: Literacy, learning and contemporary culture.* Cambridge, UK: Polity Press.

Heiligmann, R., & Shields, V. R. (2005). Media literacy, visual syntax, and magazine advertisements: Conceptualizing the consumption of reading by media literate subjects. *Journal of Visual Literacy, 25*(1), 41–66.

Hobbs, R., & Jensen, A. (2009). The past, present, and future of media literacy education. *Journal of Media Literacy Education, 1,* 1–11.

Messaris, P. (1997). *Visual persuasion: The role of images in advertising.* Thousand Oaks, CA: Sage.

Morgan, S. J. (2005). More than pictures?: An exploration of visually dominant magazine ads as arguments. *Journal of Visual Literacy, 25*(2), 145–166.

Scott, L. M. (1994). Images in advertising: The need for a theory of visual rhetoric. *Journal of Consumer Research, 21,* 252–273.

Semali, L. (2003). Ways with visual languages: Making the case for critical media literacy. *The Clearing House, 39*(3), 271–277.

Williamson, J. (1978). *Decoding advertisements: Ideology and meaning in advertising.* London: Marion Boyars.

National Association for Media Literacy Education: http://namle.net

Frank Baker's Website: http://www.frankwbaker.com

Exploring News Reports

Central Focus of the Unit

This unit focuses on the images, primarily photographic in nature, that make up the visual aspects of print-based news reports. It is important for students to understand how various images and textual elements work together to create news reports because this process is an important aspect of media literacy education. Photography has been used as a form of evidence regarding people, actions, and events for over 100 years. Iconic images from news reports (for example, Neil Armstrong walking on the moon, the assassination of President Kennedy, and the attacks on the World Trade Center) have had a tremendous impact on how we view the world and our national identity.

Photography means "to write with light", referring to the process whereby light-sensitive film or digital sensors are used to capture the light that enters the camera through a particular lens. Light is captured the instant the shutter in a camera is released, generating a realistic depiction of the events as seen through the lens. The sheer ubiquity of photographic images often conceals their constructed nature as a representational medium. In other words, they seem to be objective representations of the world because they resemble the way we see the world with our eyes. Because photographs always carry with them a referent to the world being captured in the camera, they are often erroneously assumed to be a literal and true account of actual events.

Photographic images offer an illusion of reality (Howells, 2003). They have been used in news reporting due to their resemblance to the ways humans perceive the world. Although photographic images can be easily manipulated using current technology, the news photo still offers an evidentiary warrant that drawings, paintings, and other modes cannot. Photographic images may distort reality, but there is always a presumption that something exists or did exist in reality and that something is the actual subject of the photographic image (Sontag, 1973). In other words, most photographs are a constructed reference to the world depicted.

For many years, photographic images have appeared in both digital and print formats on the front pages of newspapers and the covers of magazines. The images in these reports are accompanied by written text in the form of narrative descriptions, captions, and headlines. At times, what is offered through the photographic image enhances the information provided in the narrative description, and at other times it may stand in contradiction to what is offered in the written narrative.

Captions and other textual elements have been referred to as *anchors*, devices that help reader-viewers anchor the meaning of an image (Barthes, 1977b). Captions can label things in an image that are not named, and call attention to certain aspects of an image over others. How news is reported in visual forms and in written language is different. Different modes work in different ways, using different materials. It is the multimodal aspects of news reports, the way images and written language work, both in concert and independently, that are the focus of this unit of study.

Cornerstone Text or Visual Image

Any featured article or headline that includes a visual image taken from a local, regional, national, or international newspaper or magazine can be used as a cornerstone text for this unit. Blending some iconic photographic images from the past with some current headlines and images from today's newspapers or magazines would create a nice juxtaposition for students to consider. In addition, blending older photographs that were created on film with digitally created contemporary images might provide another avenue for comparing and contrasting.

Learning Objectives

- Explore how photographs are used in news reporting and identify several distinctive news photo genres, for example the portrait, the sports or action photo, or the context shot.
- Demonstrate to students how to identify and critique stereotypes in news images.
- Identify and analyze recurrent themes and symbols from news reports.
- Understand the concept of perspective or point of view in the photographic process and how it is used to manipulate photographic images.
- Analyze the ways written descriptions of news events are similar and different from how these events are depicted in photographs and other visual images.

Launching the Unit

To launch the unit of study on news images, teachers should gather a sizeable selection of news reports and images to consider, in both print and digital formats. Students need to be exposed to a wide variety of news images if they are going to develop a sense for how these images are used. Once they are gathered, identify and categorize these reports into subgenres or content categories, for example political events, sporting events, or daily news reports. To launch this unit, teachers should address the extent to which photographs are used across numerous news reports, and to focus more intensely on a few particular images.

After organizing the collection of images, select an image and analyze it according to the following concepts:

- *Literal Image:* Give a brief description of the literal details of the photograph.
- *Accompanying Text:* Consider the title or caption of the photograph. Is there any accompanying text that indicates particular meanings or contexts?
- *Point of View:* Where was the camera positioned to take this image?
- *Sites of Production:* Who produced the image and for what purpose? How does the production affect how we view the image?
- *Sites of Reception.* Where are you viewing the image? In what context did you encounter the image?
- *Gaze:* Do the primary subjects look at other subjects or objects or at the viewer? How does this affect your interpretation?

Analyzing various images according to these concepts helps students understand the roles, contexts of production and reception, and the structures upon which these images and news reports are constructed.

Lessons and Learning Experiences

1. *Comparing Images and Perspectives*—Collect five or more versions of a single news event from a variety of sources. The more diverse the versions of the event, the better. Utilizing different international newspapers, for example, collect reports of the same event across different geographical and political regions. Discuss how the versions of events differ and how they are the same. Why do you think these versions were constructed by the various news sources? How does the producer affect what is being produced? Ask students what is being depicted, how it is being depicted, and what made them interpret the image in that manner.

2. *Comparing Covers*—Gather together a year's worth of magazine covers from a particular magazine, for example *Time, GQ, Seventeen, Vogue,* or *Sports Illustrated*. Another way to compare covers would be to select several covers from different decades. These covers are usually available on publishers' websites. Conduct a content analysis of the covers, counting how often there are people on the cover, whether they are male or female, of what race or ethnicity, how they are posed, and what they are doing. What and who is being depicted? What is being left out? What do these covers say about the readership of the magazine? Is there anything troubling about the way humans and objects are depicted?

3. *Winners and Losers*—Collect images of sports figures, teams, or politicians who have just won or lost or game or an election. Create a double entry chart comparing the two types of images: winners and losers. What do you notice about the way the teams or persons are depicted when they win or lose? Winners tend to look up to the sky or heavens, while losers tend to look down at the ground. Winners are usually with other people rejoicing, while losers are often depicted in solitude. Are there any images that break from these norms?

4. *Emotional Images*—Select several emotions, for example sad, happy, angry, bored, or excited, and have students find images they think depict these emotions. Compare the images students select and discuss why these images were chosen and how they related to the selected emotion.

5. *Iconic Images*—Select several famous, iconic images. I suggest the *Migrant Mother* photograph by Dorothea Lange because there is so much written about it. Have students share what the image makes them think about and what it makes them feel is being portrayed. Then conduct some research into how the image was made, processed, and disseminated. For example, learning that the U.S. government commissioned this image changes how we might interpret it. Many famous news images have interesting histories that reveal more about the image when researched.

Culminating Projects

One of the more obvious culminating experiences available would be to have students use digital cameras to create news reports of events happening at school or in the local community. Creating class and school-based newspapers can be an extensive project, but one that can be educational across numerous content areas and literacy skills. In addition, students can use photo manipulation software to change the perspectives and features of photographic images. Helping students understand how processing can alter perspective is an important concept in media literacy education.

Text Sets

For this text set I offer a list of some of the top-selling, award-winning magazines produced for children:

- *National Geographic for Kids*
- *Cicada*
- *Muse*
- *Story Box*
- *Ranger Rick*
- *Dig*

- *Sports Illustrated for Kids*
- *Time for Kids*
- *Odyssey*
- *Chirp* Magazine
- *Calliope*
- *Highlights*
- *Creative Kids* Magazine
- *Owl* Magazine
- *Know—The Science Magazine for Curious Kids*
- *Humpty Dumpty*
- *Jack and Jill*

Analysis Guide: News Reports

Some Initial Questions

- What is your immediate impression of the image? What feelings does the image evoke in you?
- Describe the people in the image. Analyze the body language of the individuals or the group.
- What memories or experiences does the image stir in you? How do you identify with the people in the image?

Considering the Site of Production:

- Where was the image captured? Is it a common, recognizable place or unique?
- Who was the photo made for?
- What technologies were employed?
- What was the purpose of the photo?

Considering the Image Itself:

- What is being shown? What is the subject of the photo?
- How is the image bordered?
- What is the perspective or vantage point of the photo?
- Is the photo monochromatic or color?
- How are objects arranged? Candid? Staged?
- What symbols or figurative elements are represented?

Considering the Site of Reception:

- Who might be the intended audience of the photo?
- Where is the photo viewed? Museum? Web? Photo album?
- How is the photo circulated?
- What is the relationship between subject and viewer? Offer? Demand?

Technological Considerations:

- How does/did exposure affect the image?
- Can you tell if the image was digitally manipulated?
- Was the credibility of the image put in question by its production?

Considering the Visual Elements of a Photograph:

- *Focus:* Which areas appear clearest or sharpest in the photograph? Which do not?
- *Light:* What does the lighting suggest for the news image? Does the photograph allow you to guess the time of day? Is the light natural or artificial? Harsh or soft? Reflected or direct?
- *Repetition:* Are there any objects, shapes, or lines that create a pattern?
- *Shape:* Do you see geometric or organic shapes? What are they?
- *Space:* Is there depth to the photograph or does it seem shallow? What creates this appearance? Are there important negative spaces in addition to positive spaces? Is there depth created by spatial illusions?
- *Angle:* What is the vantage point from which the photograph was taken? Is it an unusual or exaggerated vantage point?
- *Foreground and Background:* What part of the image is foregrounded? What part of the image seems to be toward the back?
- *Central focus:* What object or objects appear most prominently and/or most clearly focused in a photograph?
- *Composition:* How are the various components of the image arranged?
- *Framing:* What has the photographer placed within the boundaries of the photograph, and what has possibly been omitted?

Further Resources

Chauvin, B. A. (2003). Visual or media literacy? *Journal of Visual Literacy, 23*(2), 119–128.

Howells, R. (2003). *Visual culture.* Malden, MA: Blackwell.

Messaris, P. (1994). *Visual literacy: Image, mind, & reality.* Boulder, CO: Westview Press.

Serafini, F. (2011). Expanding perspectives for comprehending visual images in multimodal texts. *Journal of Adolescent & Adult Literacy, 54*(5), 342–350.

Sontag, S. (1973). *On photography.* New York: Doubleday.

Sturken, M., & Cartwright, L. (2001). *Practices of looking: An introduction to visual culture.* Oxford: Oxford University Press.

Watkins, J. K., Miller, E., & Brubaker, D. (2004). The role of the visual image: What are students really learning from pictorial representations? *Journal of Visual Literacy, 24*(1), 23–40.

Exploring Film

Central Focus of the Unit

This unit will take us in a new direction as we branch out from viewing single still images to engaging with moving images or film. There are three basic components teachers and students have to consider in order to understand how films work: image, movement, and sound. Throughout this unit, we will focus on variety of film techniques, including camera placement, or angle; lighting; panning, or how the camera moves; how time is portrayed; framing, or what is included in the shot; and editing, or how the various scenes change. We will also need to address sound effects, dialogue, and background music, or soundtracks.

Most of our students have grown up watching films. They probably have seen hundreds of them by the time they reach high school. Whether they have taken an interest in how films are produced and disseminated, or have learned some techniques for analyzing them, however, is doubtful. Like advertisements, most students have spent their lives looking at films, but few have taken the time to understand how they may affect their perceptions of themselves, how they view others, and how they understand the world around them. Helping students evolve from passive recipients of film to active, critical viewers is the focus of this unit.

Film, like other media, is not a neutral representation of reality. Film offers a director's, producer's, and actor's version of reality with all the inherent biases, values, and stereotypes associated with any single perspective. *Auteur theory* suggests that the film is essentially a director's vision brought to life. This theory holds that the director's vision will shine through the studio's interference and allows for his personal imprint on a particular film. Although this theory has been contested throughout the years for overemphasizing the role of the director, it explains how particular perspectives on reality are offered through this medium.

Two important aspects of how visual images are used in film are *mise-en-scene* and framing. *Mise-en-scene* is French for "put in the scene" and includes all the props, actors, costumes, location, lighting, and dialogue used in making films. *Framing* is concerned with how all of these components are captured on film, what is included, what is left out, how the camera is positioned, and what lenses are used. Framing determines the overall composition of a film.

The biggest difference between analyzing film and analyzing still photographs is movement. There are two types of movement in film that should be considered: *continuous*—how people and objects move within a scene, and *discontinuous*—how movement is portrayed across scenes, in most cases a result of film editing. One of the challenging aspects of analyzing film, much like the challenge of comprehending the role that the gutter plays in comics and graphic novels, is understanding what happens between scenes. The transitions produced during the editing process are gaps created in the film that must be inferred by the viewer. In some transitions, the setting or time will change, and in others the perspective will change.

Helping students understand how multiple narrators and perspectives are used in postmodern picturebooks and how transitions occur in the gutters of graphic novels may support students' interpretive skills for viewing and analyzing film. Since analyzing film may be new to many students, drawing upon the strategies they have used to make sense of still images and picturebooks supports their development in this new medium.

Cornerstone Text or Visual Image

One of the most analyzed films of all time is probably *Citizen Kane*, directed by Orson Welles. This black and white classic alone is a course in camera work and framing. There is a great deal of writing available to support teachers' and students' analysis of this classic film. Another classic that has plenty of resources for analysis would be *The Wizard of Oz*, which may be a more appropriate choice for younger audiences.

In addition, there are certainly many contemporary films that can be used to launch this unit. One of the biggest challenges will be selecting quality films that are appropriate for a particular grade level. The Internet Movie Data Base (IMDB) is an excellent resource for finding quality films to view and analyze.

Learning Objectives

- Develop an understanding of the basic elements used in filmmaking, including movement, image, and sound.
- Demonstrate how changing the camera angle can affect the perspective of the viewer and the meaning potential of an action or a particular scene.
- Understand how the editing process works and how edits can change the sequence of a narrative and the time frame being presented.
- Analyze how *heroes* and *villains* and other stereotypes may be constructed in film.
- Develop a sense of the techniques filmmakers use to create mood and emotional impact on their audiences through the use of lighting, camera angle, sound, and dialogue.

Launching the Unit

Over the years, administrators have condemned watching movies in school as a waste of time, and in some cases rightly so. However, having students watch short clips taken from different movies in order to analyze and discuss them is an important aspect of media literacy education. Unfortunately, the amount of time it takes to watch full-length films is probably not available each day in school. However, the techniques used in short films are similar to the ones used in feature films. Helping students analyze short films and portions of films will help them attend to the longer ones they view on their own. Helping students evolve from passive viewers of film to active participants who analyze how stories are presented is an essential objective of this unit.

After selecting a particular film to watch, take your time to work through the opening credits to discuss how a film is launched. Did the credits roll first? Did the movie begin with an action-packed scene? How and when were the major characters introduced?

Film can be analyzed across a variety of dimensions:

1. *literary*—narration, characters, setting, themes, and symbolism;
2. *cinematic*—camera position, sound, lighting, set decoration;
3. *dramatic*—costumes, acting, blocking, makeup; and
4. *ideological*—perspectives assumed, cultural norms and biases, and value markers.

One way to help students learn to analyze a film is to watch portions a few times and take some initial notes. Then, watch the film clip again with the sound turned down so students can concentrate on the visual aspects of the film. Then, listen to the soundtrack of the movie without watching it. Many film soundtracks are readily available to listen to apart from the film itself. Students can discuss what emotions are brought forth through the music, or how the camera angle demonstrates the perspective of the film's director or characters, or how lighting adds to the emotional effect of the film.

Lessons and Learning Experiences

1. *Examining Still Images*—In order to understand how films are constructed it is often helpful to begin by analyzing a single image or shot. After some still images of the film have been discussed, watch a portion of the film with the sound turned off to focus students' attention on the visual images, movement, editing techniques, and framing. How do the individual scenes compare with one another? How many different settings are used? Does the entire film take place in one location or in many? What camera angles are used to present the narrative?

2. *Comparing Comic Heroes*—This lesson analyzes how comic books that contain a superhero like Batman, Superman, or Spider-Man are translated into movies. The comic book serves as a storyboard for understanding how a story is laid out, in much the same manner as storyboards are used in film production. How are superheroes portrayed in comic books as compared with films? What aspects of the stories that originate in comic books are left out of feature films?

3. *Examining Sounds*—Films utilize three types of sound: dialogue, sound effects, and music. Have students listen to portions of the film without seeing the images. What mood is elicited by the chosen music and sound effects? Is there dialogue in every scene, or are some scenes rather quiet? Is there a soundtrack or is it just the noises from the actions of the scene? How is music selected or created for a film? How are full songs used in the film? Why do you think these were selected?

4. *The Bechdel Test*—In 1985, Alison Bechdel described a test in her comic strip *Dykes to Watch Out For* to examine the roles that females play in film. She posed the following three questions: (1) Does a movie contain two or more female characters that have names? (2) Do the characters talk to each other or just to men? (3) Do the characters discuss things other than men? Have students use these three questions to consider the role that females play in the movies they select and watch.

5. *Positioning*—Films position the audience to consider the world and the events portrayed from a particular perspective. Helping students identify the "implied viewer" of a film helps them understand how they are possibly being manipulated by a film's content and techniques. Whom do you side with or relate to in the film? Whom do you side against?

Culminating Projects

Depending upon your background with video technology and movie software, having your students write, direct, and edit a short movie would be an excellent project for this unit. Another possibility would be to create a place for students to review films and publish those reviews online or in a class book for other students to read and use.

Text Sets

The IMDB—Internet Movie Database—is an important resource for surveying the range and genres of film. This searchable database can be accessed online or from apps available for smart phones and tablets.

Analysis Guide: Film

- Consider the title and any images associated with the film (posters, DVD cover images, advertisements).
- Watch a trailer for the movie if available. What is highlighted about the film in the trailer? How does the trailer "tease you" to watch the film?
- What do you know or have heard about the film before you watch it?

Opening:

- How does the film begin?
- What is the setting of the film? Time and place?
- What is used to introduce the characters and plot?
- Mise-en-scene—What goes into the production? Costumes? Sets? Lighting? Props?

Editing & Camera Work:

- How does the editing add to the story? Many cuts and edits or long scenes with fewer cuts?
- Camera positions? How do we see the scenes?
- How are individual scenes ended? Fades? Dissolves? Abrupt cuts? etc.

Sound:

- Is there a laugh track?
- Is there music during the movie? How does this add to the story?
- Are recognizable songs used in the soundtrack?
- What sound effects are used? How does this add to the story?
- Is sound linked to the images or does it carry over from image to image?
- What role does silence play in the movie?

Point of View:

- How is the camera used to show a point of view?
- Who is telling the story and how is this shown?
- Who is narrating the movie? How does this affect the story?

Themes:

- Who are the central characters? What might each character represent?
- What kind of life or actions does the film want you to value? Criticize?
- Is there a coherent message or moral in the movie? If not, why not?
- How does the movie make you feel at the end? Have your views changed through the movie?

Further Resources

Baker, F. W. (2012). *Media literacy in the K–12 classroom*. Eugene, OR: International Society for Technology in Education.

Beach, R. (2007). *Teachingmedialiteracy.com: A web-linked guide to resources and activities*. New York: Teachers College.

Corrigan, T. J. (2007). *A short guide to writing about film*. New York: Pearson.

Mitry, J., & King, C. T. (2000). *Semiotics and the analysis of film*. Bloomington: Indiana University Press.

Stafford, T. (2011). *Teaching visual literacy in the primary classroom: Comic books, film, television and picture narratives*. London: Routledge.

www.imdb.com
www.filmeducation.org
www.filmsite.org

Exploring Digital Media

Central Focus of the Unit

A primary goal of digital media education is to foster active, critical response to various media, as opposed to passive participation (Beach, 2007). It is important for students to understand how digital media affects their emerging identities and constructs their social and cultural realities. As the types of media that students encounter continually evolve into digitally based resources, teachers need to provide students with the tools for considering the contexts and technologies for how media is produced, disseminated, and accessed.

This unit of study will serve as a sort of collective, addressing a variety of digital media not addressed in previous units of study. Wikis, weblogs, podcasts, websites, social media platforms like Facebook and Twitter, and other digital resources attract a growing percentage of our students' online attention. One of the primary challenges of discussing these digital resources is how quickly they come and go. By the time this book is published, some of the popular online resources mentioned above may have changed or lessened in importance only to be replaced by new ones. Because of this rapid turnover, many of these online resources can be discussed only in general terms.

One of the most important distinctions involved with digital media is the shift from what has been called Web 1.0 to Web 2.0 (Lankshear & Knobel, 2006). In a Web 1.0 environment, the information provided was produced by the few for the consumption of the many. An extensive array of Web 1.0 resources were made available through the Internet for people to retrieve information created by experts, organizations, educational institutions, corporations, and government entities. In a Web 2.0 environment, the distinction between consumer and producer of information, author and reader, novice and expert has been blurred. Today, any person with a computer or smart phone and an Internet connection can produce information for anyone interested in accessing it. Students now have easy access to university lectures, the Library of Congress' bank of images, museum exhibits, historical archives, and a wide assortment of what was once only available to privileged individuals as print-based or analog resources. The shift from Web 1.0 to Web 2.0 has forever changed education and how our students access the world.

In addition to changes to the content made available on the Web, drastic changes have also taken place regarding the technologies used to access, store, and organize this ever-expanding content. Web-based resources that were originally created by a single person or small groups of people have been changed through technologies like wikis, Google Docs, and YouTube to allow millions of people to generate content on the Internet. The power that once resided in the hands of a few people has now been distributed across many, providing access and opportunity for traditionally marginalized groups.

To be able to understand and discuss these changes, we have to address not only *what* has been made available, but also *how* it is made available. Questions of copyright and ownership of content have accompanied the proliferation of information on the Internet and will be important issues throughout our students' lives. As we help students learn to access information through new technologies, issues of privacy, ownership, and personal freedom become more and more relevant. Not only do we need to teach students how to use new technologies, we need to help them understand the benefits and challenges that these new technologies offer.

Cornerstone Text or Visual Image

There are so many examples of digital media available, selecting a single resource to examine over all the other possible resources available would be limiting. To begin, teachers need to avail themselves of the wide range of digital resources available. One possible way to introduce this unit of study is by asking students which media sites and digital resources they are currently using. The ubiquitous presence of Facebook makes it an obvious digital media resource to begin with. However, we often relegate social media sites to a lower class of digital resource due to its content and informality. Twitter, YouTube, Pinterest, Second Life, Tumblr, and Edmodo are all possible resources to investigate initially. Select a digital resource and spend some time working with it and researching it yourself before introducing it to your students.

Learning Objectives

- Help students learn how to access information using a variety of digital media resources.
- Teach students some basic techniques for analyzing the messages disseminated through various digital media and resources.
- Provide techniques for students to determine the credibility of various digital media and resources.
- Demonstrate how media are constructed representations of information, opinions, and reality. Help students determine the perspectives offered and how to locate alternative or competing information and opinions.

- Support students as they begin to develop the skills and strategies for creating their own digital resources using a wide array of digital technologies.

Launching the Unit

After surveying students' knowledge of various digital media, select one to use as a demonstration of how to access and analyze the information or resources made available through this particular technology. Before trying to demonstrate any new technologies to students, teachers need to work with these resources so they have a better sense of what these technologies can do and how they operate.

Selecting one particular digital resource, allow students time to explore the resource, roaming around its design to get a better sense of how it works before formally analyzing it. It takes time to become comfortable with any of these resources, and we want students to be successful when they begin. Use the instructions or video guides as a resource to demonstrate to students what is possible with each resource. Trying to get them to envision what their own productions might look like is an important first step.

One of the primary goals of this unit is to demonstrate how media resources are value statements that reflect particular biased interests, not neutral, objective presentations of facts. As we begin to explore the various resources outlined in this unit, we need to ensure we remain skeptical and teach our students to remain equally skeptical about the information and resources provided. As stated elsewhere, developing critically aware, active consumers of information and media messages is an essential component of media literacy education.

Lessons and Learning Experiences

1. *Assessing Credibility*—One of the most important lessons in this unit is helping students assess the quality and credibility of the information they explore in online environments. If you search the Internet for the keywords *Pacific Northwest Tree Octopus*, you will be able to access a site that was produced to help students evaluate the credibility of information on the Internet. This website was created in 1998 by Lyle Zapato as an elaborate hoax, posing as a legitimate educational resource. On the actual website there is no indication that the information is bogus. It is only through examination of the links and information provided on other websites that students are able to see through the façade. Distinguishing facts from opinions or identifying misinformation requires more than careful reading of a single resource. It requires the examination of numerous resources, weighing evidence and coming to one's own conclusions.

2. *Podcasts*—Podcasts are an important resource for sharing information in visual, audio, and video formats. Made available through the Apple iTunes

website and other Internet platforms, podcasts are recorded files made available for free or cheaply for people to download and access on portable media players or computers. Prominent universities now make available millions of recorded lectures for free. There are software programs that allow students to easily create podcasts and make them available online. I have used a software program called ProfCast that allows me to share PowerPoint slides that accompany my audio-based lectures.

3. *Creating Blogs and Wikis*—Two of the easiest and most powerful digital resources available are blogs and wikis. Blogs or weblogs are personal, journal-like web resources students can use to share their ideas and writing online. Wikis are used by groups of people to create documents collaboratively. Wikipedia is a well-known example of a collaborative use of wiki technology. The most important aspect of these online resources is their social and communal aspect. No longer are students required to write journal entries for the sole audience of their teachers. Rather, they can publish their ideas online for other students to read and respond. These blogs and wikis also make linking to other web-based resources very easy, allowing students to automatically search for associated resources, visual images, and news feeds. Students can also select a particular blog or wiki to follow and share with the class.

4. *Book Review Sites*—There are numerous websites for sharing what students are reading with people from all over the world. I have used the site goodreads.com in my children's literature courses for years. Two other book club and review sites that are popular are Shelfari.com and LibraryThing.com. All three of these sites are free and easy to navigate. Have students create an account on one site and begin to share their comments and reviews about the books they are reading. These sites can be managed for levels of privacy, and groups can be created that are kept private from other readers. I think these sites can take the place of the reading response notebooks that I have used in my classroom for many years.

5. *Follow a Resource*—Have students sign up on Twitter, Tumblr, or a news website to follow a particular educational institution. Have students select a resource that is updated frequently so they will get new information on a regular basis. Students can be organized in small groups to share their resources based on areas of interest.

Culminating Projects

As suggested by the shift from Web 1.0 to Web 2.0, students are no longer simply consumers of information; they are also producers and disseminators. The creation of blogs, wikis, book reviews, websites, and podcasts is an important culminating experience. These creations help students understand the power of online media to provide access to information and share content. Teachers may have to enlist help with some of the technology aspects of these projects. Creating online, digitally based resources has become much easier in the past few years, allowing more teachers and students to access and create information and make it available. The more comfortable teachers become with some of this technology, the better able they will be to support students' development in media literacy skills and provide access to different tools for sharing ideas.

Text Sets

For this text set, I will be sharing some of my favorite online resources. I have selected those sites that seem popular and solid enough to be around long past this publication, but there are no guarantees.

Digital Media Resources:

http://www.tumblr.com
http://www.goodreads.com
http://www.librarything.com
https://twitter.com
http://www.shelfari.com
http://pinterest.com
https://www.stumbleupon.com
http://www.ning.com
http://www.edmodo.com
http://www.jacketflap.com
http://www.flickr.com
http://www.screencast.com
http://voicethread.com
http://www.diigo.com
http://www.wikispaces.com

Digital Media Literacy Education Resources:

http://www.medialit.org
http://medialiteracyproject.org
http://namle.net
http://www.medialiteracy.com
http://teachingmedialiteracy.com

Analysis Guide: Digital Media

Consider Sites of Production:

- Who created this digital media? Is it a commercial or public enterprise?
- When was this resource made available?
- What is the purpose of this type of media?
- Who runs the site or paid for the production?
- What digital technologies were used in its creation?

Consider the Message/Media Itself:

- What is the content of the source or media?
- How is the content presented?
- What is the proposed message?
- What lifestyles, values, and perspectives are represented?
- Has any important information been left out? Might this omission be intentional?
- Whose values are implied by this source? Whose values are not?
- What links are available? How are these sources connected?

Consider the Sites of Reception?

- Who is the intended audience?
- How is the information made available? Is it a pay-per-view site or free?
- How credible is the information provided?
- What sources are listed as an authority for these resources?

Further Resources

Baker, F. W. (2012). *Media literacy in the K–12 classroom.* Eugene, OR: International Society for Technology in Education.

Beach, R. (2007). *Teachingmedialiteracy.com: A web-linked guide to resources and activities.* New York: Teachers College.

Hobbs, R. (2011). *Digital and media literacy: Connecting culture and classroom.* Thousand Oaks, CA: Corwin Press.

Richardson, W. (2009). *Blogs, wikis, podcasts and other powerful web tools for classrooms.* Thousand Oaks, CA: Corwin Press.

Epilogue: To See or Not to See

> The real voyage of discovery consists not in seeking new landscapes
> but in having new eyes.
>
> —Marcel Proust (1932)

In the opening epigraph, Proust calls for people to seek new ways of seeing, not simply new things to see. In much the same manner, the focus of this book has been to help teachers and students develop new strategies and practices that foster a different way of seeing, a more intentional way for students to navigate, interpret, and analyze visual images and multimodal ensembles.

Earlier in this book, references were made to a particular *way of seeing*. Berger (1972) differentiated between *looking* and *seeing*, suggesting the concept of seeing went beyond merely perceiving to include interpretation. Gombrich (1961) suggested the *innocent eye is blind*. Goodman (1976) asserted *the eye always comes ancient to its work*. These statements all refer to a particular way of seeing that encompasses interpretation and critical inquiry into the meaning potential of visual images and multimodal ensembles. The development of a *critical eye* is the essence of this monograph.

The concept of an *enlightened eye* comes from one of my favorite books on qualitative research and inquiry, *The Enlightened Eye* by Eisner (1998). In this book, Eisner, an artist and arts-based researcher, suggested we as educators need to find new and enlightened ways to see and experience the events that surround our lives as teachers. Eisner (1998) states, "Critics have the formidable task of making sense of some of the most complicated and subtle works that humans have created—works of art" (p. 3). I suggest the same formidable task is associated with the visual images and multimodal texts that students encounter and try to make sense of each and every day, both in and out of school settings. It is our duty as literacy educators to demonstrate more subtle and nuanced ways of experiencing the images and multimodal ensembles in our students' lives, helping them to make deeper sense of these complicated texts.

In essence, an enlightened eye is a form of *visual criticism*. Unfortunately, the word *criticism* often carries negative connotations, suggesting it is a process of ridiculing or finding fault with someone or something. I prefer Eisner's definition of criticism, which states, "Criticism is an art of saying useful things about complex and subtle objects and events so that others less sophisticated, or sophisticated in different ways, can see and understand what they did not see and understand before" (p. 3). It is my hope that we can venture forth as literacy educators and find some useful things to say about visual images and multimodal ensembles.

DEVELOPING AN ENLIGHTENED EYE WITH OUR STUDENTS

As Gombrich (1972) so eloquently states, "Reading can never be a passive affair" (p. 86). Students need to become active in their search for understanding and ever diligent to avoid reaching closure prematurely before all possible perspectives have been considered. In the spirit of critical thinking, we need to demonstrate to our students our willingness to wrestle with the various meaning potentials available, thinking again and again about what is possible, not simply what is obvious.

Our role as the facilitators of students' learning experiences in our classrooms is based on the concept of *scaffolding*. A scaffold is a structure erected in parallel to a building to support its construction or remodeling. In much the same way teachers work in parallel with students to support their construction of meaning and interpretations. Sipe (2008) described effective scaffolding as the application of multiple roles by a teacher, a focus on multiple interpretations rather than comprehension, a shift in the way teachers and students are allowed to discuss texts, the nature of the text being interpreted, and a sociocultural context where each reader supports one another.

Our discussions with students about the visual images, written narratives, and design elements in the multimodal ensembles we explore together build scaffolds and create *space* where students may evolve into interpreters of these texts. It is in this space that we demonstrate what it means to be a successful reader and how readers explore the meaning potentials of the texts and images they encounter.

WORDS AND PICTURES AND SOMETHING IN BETWEEN

When Arizpe and Styles (2003) asked Anthony Browne about the role of words and pictures in his picturebooks, he replied that both were important, but added, "And some things you say in the gap between the words and the pictures" (p. 207). This book has been an attempt to understand what happens in the words and images as well as the *gap between* suggested by Browne. Understanding how various modes work individually is important, but what is essential is coming to see how various modes work in concert with one another as elements of a multimodal ensemble. There is a synergistic relationship among the elements of a multimodal ensemble, suggesting the meaning of the total ensemble is greater than the sum of its constituent parts.

INTERPRETATION AND REPRESENTATION

Basically, there are two primary semiotic processes at work: interpretation and representation. An inwardly conceived sign is an interpretation, and an outwardly realized sign is a representation. Humans use a variety of representations to archive their existence, share their ideas, and explore their inner worlds. When we come to see all the modes available to humans to represent their ideas, we realize how versatile we are at making sense of the world. We as educators need to remember that sometimes it is just that simple: interpretation and representation.

THE JOURNEY CONTINUES

As the resources we have for interpreting and representing ideas continue to expand, our pedagogical framework for teaching students to make sense of these resources must continue to expand as well. As teachers, we ourselves need to explore the various multimodal ensembles our students will encounter before we are effectively positioned to demonstrate the strategies and skills necessary for navigating and analyzing these texts and supporting students' engagement in more meaningful ways. Literacy education is changing rapidly; we need to expand our own knowledge base and skill set if we are to remain viable facilitators of our students' literacy development.

Glossary

Aptness: A sense of how well a particular mode fits a designer's intentions.

Connotation: The sociocultural or personal meanings a person brings to an image or text. The connotative meanings extend beyond the literal or denotative level.

Denotation: The definitional, obvious, or literal meaning of a text or image. Some theorists have suggested denotation and connotation are separate meanings, but others have found this distinction problematic.

Design elements: Aspects of a multimodal ensemble that include borders, fonts, spatial arrangements, and graphic designs. This term is used to refer to elements of a multimodal ensemble beyond the visual images and printed text.

Framing: Setting off particular aspects of a multimodal ensemble or the world through visual and textual devices. Framing devices establish boundaries between various aspects of multimodal ensembles. Punctuation in written language, borders around paintings, and endpapers in picturebooks all establish frames around modal entities.

Iconography: A branch of the visual arts concerned with the themes and meaning potentials of various art forms. Iconographical analysis involves the identification, description, and interpretation of the content of visual images, for example the subjects depicted and particular compositional elements that are distinct from artistic style.

Iconology: The branch of art history that deals with the description, analysis, and interpretation of icons or iconic representations.

Ideational metafunction: Also referred to as the representational metafunction, the ideational metafunction involves aspects of language and visual images that carry meaning potential. Based on the work of Halliday, it is one of the three metafunctions of language, interpersonal and textual being the other two.

Ideology: A set of socially constructed ways of thinking and acting that become embedded and naturalized in a particular culture, to the extent that they become invisible or common sense. A set of conscious and unconscious ideas that constitute one's worldview or ways of looking at things that affects the meanings people construct.

Interpersonal metafunction: Aspects of language that set up relationships among speakers and listeners. It refers to how language and visual images establish relationships between producers and receivers. Based on the work of Halliday, it is one of the three metafunctions of language, ideational and textual being the other two.

Materiality: The concept that all modes are made up of particular materials providing certain affordances and limitations due to their material aspects.

Meaning potential: The possible meanings a particular sign, symbol, word, or visual image evokes. This term is used to suggest the association between signs and meaning is not direct, singular, or stable. Because particular meanings are not fixed, nor stable, individuals can revise and renegotiate these meanings with others.

Media: The particular technologies used for the rendering and dissemination of texts, in particular multimodal ensembles. For example, television, radio, the Internet, electronic books, and DVDs are all types of media.

Media literacy: The ability to critically understand, question, and evaluate how media work to produce meanings, and how they organize, mediate, and construct reality.

Metafunction: Aspects of language and visual images that make it possible to communicate across time and space. Metafunctions are aspects of language and serve as a device for organizing how language and visual images work.

Mimetic: Representations that resemble or *mimic* the things they represent.

Modal fixing: The act of fixing a person's (rhetor's) intentions in a particular mode at a particular time.

Modality: The degree to which we are to consider the realistic or fictional qualities of an image or multimodal ensemble. A high degree of modality suggests the image is very realistic, while a low degree of modality suggests the image is very fictional or abstract.

Mode: A system of visual and verbal entities created within or across various cultures to represent and express meanings. Photography, sculpture, written language, paintings, music, and poetry are types of modes.

Multiliteracies: The reconceptualization of literacy as a multidimensional set of competencies and social practices in response to the increasing complexity and multimodal nature of texts. This concept suggests literacy is not a single, cognitive set of skills, rather an array of social practices that extend beyond reading and writing printed text.

Multimodal ensemble: A cohesive entity that uses a variety of semiotic resources, including written language, visual images, and design elements to represent and communicate ideas and meanings. A text that may occur in both print and digital environments, utilizing a variety of cultural and semiotic resources to articulate, render, represent, and communicate an array of concepts and information.

Multimodality: An interdisciplinary approach that understands representation and communication extend beyond written language and includes a multiplicity of modes. It refers to the theory that meanings are represented and communicated across and within cultures by a wide variety of semiotic resources.

Perception: An active process where the brain selects from the myriad of stimuli available based on one's interests and knowledge. It is a dynamic process in which the brain automatically filters, discards, and selects information.

Polysemous: The capacity of a word or visual image to have more than one meaning.

Rhetor: The designer or constructor of a multimodal ensemble or text. This individual selects from the possible modes of representation and creates the entity used to communicate meanings.

Salience: The degree to which an artist or illustrator is trying to catch the viewer's eye to communicate the importance of a particular object or participant in an image. It refers to the degree to which an artist wants the viewer to focus on a particular element or spatial composition in a visual image.

Semiotic resource: An umbrella term used here to refer to the various means for representing and communicating meanings. It is a material and social resource used for communicative purposes. Semiotic resources have a meaning potential, based on their past uses, and a set of affordances based on their possible uses, and these will be actualized in concrete social contexts.

Textual metafunction: Also referred to as the compositional metafunction, it refers to the way language or a visual image is organized. Based on the work of Halliday, it is one of the three metafunctions of language, ideational and interpersonal being the other two.

Visual literacy: The process of generating meanings in transaction with multimodal ensembles, including written text, visual images, and design elements, from a variety of perspectives to meet the requirements of particular social contexts.

References

Aiello, G. (2006). Theoretical advances in critical visual analysis: perception, ideology, mythologies, and social semiotics. *Journal of Visual Literacy, 26*(2), 89–102.

Albers, P. (2007). Visual discourse analysis: An introduction to the analysis of school-generated visual texts. In D. W. Rowe, R. T. Jiminez, D. L. Compton, D. K. Dickinson, Y. Kim, K. M. Leander, & V. J. Risko (Eds.), *56th Yearbook of the National Reading Conference* (pp. 81–95). Oak Creek, WI: NRC.

Albers, P. (2008). Theorizing visual representation in children's literature. *Journal of Literacy Research, 40*(2), 163–200.

Alvermann, D. E., & Hagood, M. C. (2000). Critical media literacy: Research, theory, and practice in "New Times". *The Journal of Educational Research, 93*(3), 193–205.

Anstey, M., & Bull, G. (2006). *Teaching and learning multiliteracies: Changing times, changing literacies.* Newark, DE: International Reading Association.

Arizpe, E., & Styles, M. (2003). *Children reading pictures: Interpreting visual texts.* New York: Routledge.

Arnheim, R. (1986). *Art and visual perception: A psychology of the creative eye.* Berkeley, CA: University of California Press.

Au, K. H. (1993). *Literacy instruction in multicultural settings.* Fort Worth, TX: Harcourt Brace Jovanovich.

Ausburn, J. L., & Ausburn, F. G. (1978). Visual literacy: Background, theory, and practice. *Programmed Learning & Educational Technology, 15,* 292–297.

Avgerinou, M. (2009). Re-viewing visual literacy in the "Bain d'Images" era. *TechTrends, 53*(2), 28–34.

Avgerinou, M., & Pettersson, R. (2011). Toward a cohesive theory of visual literacy. *Journal of Visual Literacy, 30*(2), 1–19.

Bader, B. (1976). *American picturebooks from Noah's ark to the Beast within.* New York: Macmillan.

Baldry, A., & Thibault, P. J. (2006). *Multimodal transcription and analysis: A multimedia toolkit and coursebook.* London: Equinox.

Bamford, A. (2003). *The visual literacy white paper.* Sydney: Adobe Systems Pty Ltd, Australia.

Bang, M. (2000). *Picture this: How pictures work.* San Francisco: Chronicle Books.

Barthes, R. (1977a). The death of the author. In R. Barthes (Ed.), *Imagee,- Music-, Text* (pp. 142–148). New York: Hill and Wang.

Barthes, R. (1977b). The rhetoric of the image. In R. Barthes (Ed.), *Imagee,- Music-, Text* (pp. 32–51). New York: Hill and Wang.

Barton, D., Hamilton, M., & Ivanic, R. (Eds.). (1999). *Situated literacies: Reading and writing in context.* London: Routledge.

Beardsley, M. C. (1981). *Aesthetics: Problems in the philosophy of criticism.* Indianapolis, IN: Hackett Publishing Company.

Bearne, E. (2003). Rethinking literacy: Communication, representation and text. *Reading: Literacy and Language, 37*(3), 98–103.

Beckett, S. (2010). Artistic allusions in picturebooks. In T. Colomer, B. Kummerling-Meibauer, & C. Silva-Diaz (Eds.), *New directions in picturebook research* (pp. 83–98). New York: Routledge.

Berger, J. (1972). *Ways of seeing.* London: Penguin.

Brumberger, E. (2011). Visual literacy and the digital native: An examination of the millennial learner. *Journal of Visual Literacy, 30*(1), 19–46.

Buckingham, D. (2003). *Media education: Literacy, learning and contemporary culture.* Cambridge, UK: Polity Press.

Chauvin, B. A. (2003). Visual or media literacy? *Journal of Visual Literacy, 23*(2), 119–128.

Cope, B., & Kalantzis, M. (2009). "Multiliteracies": New literacies, new learning. *Pedagogies: An International Journal, 4*(3), 164–195.

de Silva Joyce, H., & Gaudin, J. (2007). *Interpreting the visual: A resource book for teachers.* Putney, Australia: Phoenix Education.

Debes, J. L. (1968). Some foundations for visual literacy. *Audiovisual Instruction, 13*, 961–964.

Dondis, D. A. (1973). *A primer of visual literacy.* Cambridge, MA: MIT Press.

Doonan, J. (1993). *Looking at pictures in picture books.* Stroud, UK: Thimble Press.

Duncum, P. (2004). Visual culture isn't just visual: Multiliteracy, multimodality, and meaning. *Studies in Art Education, 45*(3), 252–264.

Eisner, E. (1998). *The enlightened eye: Qualitative inquiry and the enhancement of educational practice.* Upper Saddle River, NJ: Prentice-Hall.

Eisner, E. W. (2002). *The arts and the creation of mind.* New Haven, CT: Yale University Press.

Eisner, W. (2008). *Comics and sequential art: Principles and practices from the legendary cartoonist Will Eisner.* New York: W. W. Norton.

Elkins, J. (2008). *Visual literacy.* New York: Routledge.

Evans, D. (2008). *Show and tell: Exploring the fine art of children's book illustration.* San Francisco: Chronicle Books.

Fairclough, N. (1995). *Critical discourse analysis: The critical study of language.* London: Longman.

Feldman, E. B. (1981). *Varieties of visual experience.* Englewood Cliffs, NJ: Prentice Hall.

Fleckenstein, K. S., Calendrillo, L. T., & Worley, D. A. (Eds.). (2002). *Language and image in the reading-writing classroom: Teaching vision.* Mahwah, NJ: Erlbaum.

Fransecky, R. B., & Debes, J. L. (1972). *Visual literacy: A way to learn, a way to teach.* Washington, DC: AECT Publications.

References 175

Freire, P. (1970). *Pedagogy of the oppressed* (M. B. Ramos, Trans.). New York: Herder and Herder.

Gee, J. P. (1996). *Social linguistics and literacies: Ideology in discourses.* London: Taylor & Francis.

Gombrich, E. H. (1961). *Art and illusion: A study in the psychology of pictorial representation* (2nd ed.). Princeton, NJ: Princeton University Press.

Gombrich, E. H. (1972). The visual image. *Scientific American, 227*, 82–96.

Goodman, N. (1976). *Languages of art.* Indianapolis, IN: Hackett Publishing Company.

Graham, J. (1990). *Pictures on the page.* Exeter, UK: Short Run Press.

Hall, S. (Ed.). (1997). *Representation: Cultural representations and signifying practices.* London: Sage.

Halliday, M. A. K. (1978). *Language as social semiotic: The social interpretation of language and meaning.* London: Edward Arnold.

Harvey, S., & Goudvis, A. (2000). *Strategies that work: Teaching comprehension to enhance understanding.* Portland, ME: Stenhouse.

Hasenmueller, C. (1987). Panofsky, iconography, and semiotics. *Journal of Aesthetics and Art Criticism, 35*, 289–301.

Hobbs, R. (2011). *Digital and media literacy: Connecting culture and classroom.* Thousand Oaks, CA: Corwin Press.

Hobbs, R., & Jensen, A. (2009). "The past, present, and future of media literacy education." *Journal of Media Literacy Education 1*: 1–11.

Hodge, R., & Kress, G. (1988). *Social semiotics.* Cambridge, UK: Polity Press.

Howells, R. (2003). *Visual culture.* Malden, MA: Blackwell.

Hull, G. A., & Nelson, M. E. (2005). Locating the semiotic power of multimodality. *Written Communication, 22*(2), 224–261.

Hutcheon, L. (2000). *A theory of parody: The teaching of twentieth-century art forms.* Chicago: University of Chicago Press.

Iedema, R. (2001). Analysing film and television: A social semiotic account of *Hospital:* An unhealthy business. In T. van Leeuwen & C. Jewitt (Eds.), *Handbook of Visual Analysis* (pp. 183–204). London: Sage.

Iedema, R. (2003). Multimodality, resemiotization: Extending the analysis of discourse as multi-semiotic practice. *Visual Communication, 2*(1), 29–57.

Jewitt, C. (2006). *Technology, literacy and learning: A multimodal approach.* London: Routledge.

Jewitt, C. (Ed.). (2009). *The Routledge handbook of multimodal analysis.* London: Routledge.

Jewitt, C., & Oyama, R. (2001). Visual meaning: A social semiotic approach. In T. van Leeuwen & C. Jewitt (Eds.), *Handbook of visual analysis* (pp. 134–156). London: Sage.

Kiefer, B. (1995). *The potential of picturebooks: From visual literacy to aesthetic understanding.* Englewood Cliffs, New Jersey: Prentice-Hall.

Kress, G. (2003). *Literacy in the new media age.* London: Routledge.

Kress, G. (2004). Gains and losses: New forms of text, knowledge, and learning. *Computers and Composition, 22*, 5–22.

Kress, G. (2010). *Multimodality: A social semiotic approach to contemporary communication.* London: Routledge.

Kress, G., & van Leeuwen, T. (1996). *Reading images: The grammar of visual design*. London, UK: Routledge Falmer.

Lankshear, C., & Knobel, M. (2006). *New literacies: Everyday practices and classroom learning*. Berkshire, UK: Open University Press.

Lemke, J. L. (1998). Metamedia literacy: Transforming meanings and media. In D. Reinking (Ed.), *Literacy for the 21st century: Technological transformation in a post-typographic world* (pp. 283–301). Mahwah, NJ: Erlbaum.

Lessing, G. E. (1766/1990). Laokoon: Oder uber die grenzen der malerei und poesie. In E. Barner (Ed.), *Gotthold Ephrain Lessing-werke und briefe* (pp. 11–321). Frankfurt: Deutscher Klassiker Verlag.

Luke, C. (2000). New literacies in teacher education. *Journal of Adolescent and Adult Literacy, 43*(5), 424–435.

Machin, D. (2007). *Introduction to multimodal analysis*. London: Hodder Arnold.

Mackey, M. (2003). At play on the borders of the diegetic: Story boundaries and narrative interpretation. *Journal of Literacy Research, 35*(1), 591–632.

Marantz, S. S., & Marantz, K. A. (1988). *The art of children's picture books : A selective reference guide*. New York: Garland Pub.

Marx, K. (1930). *Capital* (P. Eden & P. Cedar, Trans.). New York: Dutton.

McCallum, R. (1996). Very advanced texts: Metafictions and experimental work. In P. Hunt (Ed.), *International companion encyclopedia of children's literature* (pp. 397–409). New York: Routledge.

McCloskey, R. (1958). Acceptance speech for *Make Way for Duckings*. In L. Kingman (Ed.), *Newbery and Caldecott Medal Books: 1956–1965, with acceptance papers, biographies & related materials chiefly from* (Vol. III). New York: Horn Book.

McCloud, S. (1994). *Understanding comics: The invisible art*. New York: Harper.

Messaris, P. (1994). *Visual literacy: Image, mind, & reality*. Boulder, CO: Westview Press.

Messaris, P. (1997). *Visual persuasion: The role of images in advertising*. Thousand Oaks, CA: Sage.

Meyrowitz, J. (1998). Multiple media literacies. *Journal of Communication, 48*(1), 96–108.

Miller, D. (2002). *Reading with meaning: Teaching comprehension in the primary grades*. Portland, ME: Stenhouse.

Mitchell, W. J. T. (1986). *Iconology: Image, text, ideology*. Chicago: University of Chicago Press.

Mitchell, W. J. T. (1994). *Picture Theory: Essays on Verbal and Visual Representation*. Chicago: University of Chicago Press.

Mitchell, W. J. T. (2005). There are no visual media. *Journal of Visual Culture, 4*(2), 257–266.

Moebius, W. (1986). Introduction to picturebook codes. *Word & Image, 2*(2), 141–158.

National Association for Media Literacy Education. NAMLE. (2007). About NAMLE. Available at www.namle.net

New London Group. (1996). A pedagogy of multiliteracies: Designing social futures. *Harvard Educational Review, 66*(1), 60–92.

Nia, I. (1999). Units of study in the writing workshop. *Primary Voices K–6, 8*(1), 3–11.

Nikolajeva, M., & Scott, C. (2006). *How picturebooks work*. New York: Routledge.

Nodelman, P. (1988). *Words about pictures: The narrative art of children's picture books*. Athens, GA: University of Georgia Press.

Norris, S. (2004). *Analyzing multimodal interaction: A methodological framework*. New York/London: Routledge.

O'Halloran, K. (Ed.). (2004). *Multimodal discourse analysis: Systemic functional perspectives*. London: Continuum.

O'Toole, M. (1994). *The language of displayed art*. Leicester, UK: Leicester University Press.

Panofsky, E. (1955). *Meaning in the visual arts*. Chicago: University of Chicago Press.

Pearson, P. D., & Gallagher, M. C. (1983). The instruction of reading comprehension. *Contemporary Educational Psychology, 8*, 317–344.

Pierce, C. S. (1960). *Collected papers Vol I & II*. Cambridge, MA: Harvard University Press.

Ray, K. W. (1999). *Wondrous words: Writers and writing in the elementary classroom*. Urbana, IL: National Council of Teachers of English.

Richardson, W. (2009). *Blogs, wikis, podcasts and other powerful web tools for classrooms*. Thousand Oaks, CA: Corwin Press.

Rose, G. (2001). *Visual methodologies*. London: Sage.

Salisbury, M. (2007). *Play pen: New children's book illustration*. London: Laurence King Publishing.

Saussure, F. D. (1910). *Course in general linguistics*. New York: McGraw-Hill.

Schirato, T., & Webb, J. (2004). *Understanding the visual*. Crows Nest NSW: Allen & Unwin.

Schwarcz, J. H., & Schwarcz, C. (1990). *The picture book comes of age: Looking at childhood through the art of illustrations*. Chicago: American Library Association.

Scollon, R., & Scollon, S. W. (2003). *Discourses in place: Language in the material world*. London: Routledge.

Semali, L. (2000). *Literacy in multimedia America: Integrating media education across the curriculum*. New York: Falmer Press.

Serafini, F. (2001). *The reading workshop: Creating space for readers*. Portsmouth, NH: Heinemann.

Serafini, F. (2004). *Lessons in comprehension: Explicit instruction in the reading workshop*. Portsmouth, NH: Heinemann.

Serafini, F. (2009). Understanding visual images in picturebooks. In J. Evans (Ed.), *Talking beyond the page: Reading and responding to contemporary picturebooks* (pp. 10–25). London: Routledge.

Serafini, F. (2010a). *Clasroom reading assessments: More efficient ways to view and evaluate your readers*. Portsmouth, NH: Heinemann.

Serafini, F. (2010b). Reading multimodal texts: Perceptual, structural and ideological perspectives. *Children's Literature in Education, 41*, 85–104.

Serafini, F. (2012). Expanding the four resources model: Reading visual and multimodal texts. *Pedagogies: An International Journal, 7*(2), 150–164.

Serafini, F., & Clausen, J. (2012). Typography as semiotic resource. *Journal of Visual Literacy, 31*(2), 12–29.

Sipe, L. R. (1998a). How picture books work: A semiotically framed theory of text-picture relationships. *Children's Literature in Education, 29*(2), 97–108.

Sipe, L. R. (1998b). Learning the language of picture books. *Journal of Children's Literature, 24*(2), 66–75.

Sipe, L. R. (2008). *Storytime: Young children's literary understanding in the classroom.* New York: Teachers College Press.

Sipe, L. R., & Pantaleo, S. (Eds.). (2008). *Postmodern picturebooks: Play, parody, and self-referentiality.* New York: Routledge.

Sontag, S. (1973). *On photography.* New York: Doubleday.

Spiegelman, A. (1986). *Maus I: A survivor's tale: My father bleeds history.* New York: Pantheon Books.

Stafford, B. M. (2008). The remaining 10 percent: The role of sensory knowledge in the age of the self-organizing brain. In J. Elkins (Ed.), *Visual literacy* (pp. 31–58). New York: Routledge.

Stockl, H. (2007). In between modes: Language and image in printed media. In E. Ventola, C. Charles, & M. Kaltenbacher (Eds.), *Perspectives on multimodality* (pp. 9–30). Amsterdam, Netherlands: John Benjamins.

Street, B. (1995). *Social literacies: Critical approaches to literacy in development, Ethnography and education.* New York: Longman.

Sturken, M., & Cartwright, L. (2001). *Practices of looking: An introduction to visual culture.* Oxford: Oxford University Press.

van Leeuwen, T. (2006). Towards a semiotics of typography. *Information Design Journal, 14*(2), 139–155.

van Leeuwen, T. (2011). *The language of color: An introduction.* New York: Routledge.

van Leeuwen, T., & Jewitt, C. (2001). *Handbook of visual analysis.* London: Sage.

van Straten, R. (1994). *An introduction to iconography.* London: Taylor & Francis.

Zeki, S. (1999). Art and the brain. *Journal of Consciousness Studies, 6*(6-7), 76–96.

Children's Literature References

Browne, A. (1986). *Piggybook.* New York: Alfred A. Knopf.

Browne, A. (2000). *Willy's pictures.* Cambridge, MA: Candlewick Press.

Browne, A. (2001). *Voices in the park.* New York: DK Publishing.

Gravett, E. (2007). *Meerkat mail.* New York: Simon & Schuster.

Percy, G. (1994). *Arthouse.* San Francisco: Chronicle Books.

Rylant, C. (1985). *The relatives came.* New York: Aladdin Paperbacks.

Sendak, M. (1963). *Where the wild things are.* New York: Harper & Row.

Stevens, J. (1995). *Tops and bottoms.* New York: Scholastic.

Van Allsburg, C. (1981). *Jumanji.* Boston: Houghton Mifflin.

Wiesner, D. (2001). *The three pigs.* New York: Clarion Books.

Yolen, J. (1987). *Owl moon.* New York: Philomel Books.

Index

Note: Page numbers followed by *f* indicate figures. *Italicized* page numbers indicate glossary terms.

About the Author

Dr. Frank Serafini is an author, illustrator, photographer, educator, musician, and an associate professor of Literacy Education and Children's Literature at Arizona State University. Frank was an elementary school teacher and literacy specialist for 12 years.

Frank has published numerous professional development books, including *The Reading Workshop, Lessons in Comprehension, Around the Reading Workshop in 180 Days,* and *Classroom Reading Assessments.* Frank has also written and illustrated a series of nonfiction picturebooks focusing on nature. The *Looking Closely* Series contains books about the desert, garden, pond, rainforest, shore, and forest. In 2009, *Looking Closely Along the Shore* won an International Reading Association Teacher's Choice Award.

Frank's website, www.frankserafini.com, is designed to support Frank's artistic and educational endeavors.